# Brennan's of Houston In Your Kitchen

Cook it up!

## bright sky press
Albany, Texas and New York, New York

Library of Congress Cataloging-in-Publication Data

Walker, Carl, 1957 –
    Brennan's of Houston in your kitchen / Carl Walker.
        p. cm.
    Includes index.
    ISBN 0-9704729-8-6 (alk.paper)
        1. Cookery, American—Louisiana style.
        2. Cookery—Texas.
        3. Brennan's of Houston
(Restaurant)  I. Title.

    TX715.2.L68 W54 2001
    641.59763—dc21
                                    2001037798


Book design by Caroline Brock
Cover design by Barry Kilner
Food and Location Photography by Mark Davis
Illustrations by Suzanne Morris
Recipe editor:  Ann Steiner
Editor:  Katie Dickie Stavinoha

Distributed by:  Sterling Publishing Co., Inc.

Printed in China

# Brennan's of Houston In Your Kitchen

## Chef Carl Walker

### Foreword by Alex Brennan-Martin

bright sky press
Albany, Texas and New York, New York

# table of contents

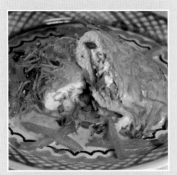

Our goal at Brennan's of Houston is to create great memories for our guests. Our customers take home no product. The taste fades and only a memory lingers.

Did we make that dining experience memorable, or did we just feed them? Man does not live by bread alone.

Since we have served about 5 million diners now, I think we are succeeding — and that success is largely because of my friend, Chef Carl Walker.

Carl knows that delivering an exceptional dining experience once is difficult, but possible. More importantly, he understands that to be truly successful, a restaurant has to deliver quality, passion and memories every meal, every day, every time. Consistency is more difficult than momentary brilliance. The reward is enduring — and the effort is certainly worthwhile.

John Mariani, the dean of American food writers, captured the reason why Carl was twice named Best Chef in Houston. "… Maybe because he is one of the few Houston chefs dedicated enough to want to be in his restaurant every night of the week, producing sumptuous food in a civilized and sophisticated atmosphere."

Maybe it's not every night because my friend is a dedicated father and family man — and the two of us do manage an occasional hunt. But, dedicated to his profession, *absolument cher!*

Carl Walker inspires people to follow him by challenging them to be their best, and working alongside them in the kitchen — even though his responsibilities span the restaurant's total operation. Carl has what I call true "followship;" people naturally gravitate toward his quiet confidence. He is also a gentleman, a commodity more uncommon today than truffles.

Carl operates with — and for — our team. He moves easily between produce growers and presidents.

My mother Ella Brennan always says that to be a success in the restaurant business: "First you make a friend."

Carl Walker evangelizes that message by continually improving our food, our service and our memory-making potential. A Will Rogers quotation on our office door reads, "Even if you are on the right track, you'll get run over if you don't keep moving." Carl epitomizes that adage. He's not afraid to try new things, but he never experiments on a customer. He is always searching for improvements, but never rests on any laurels.

He lives, and I'm sure, dreams about the restaurant. I trust his instincts.

When he decided 2001 was the right time to write a cookbook, I was strongly behind him because it's past time that Chef Carl Walker receives the accolades and the attention he's earned as one of the top chefs in the United States.

Developing this cookbook, Carl approached it in typical fashion. He's quizzed people at bookstores about their cookbook choices. He's questioned cookbook authors, tested every recipe in this book and had sous chefs re-test them. He's consulted everyday cooks and he's listened to what they've said. Carl told me that he would only consider this book a success if he got to "sign some with pages that were stained and dirty." That may say more about who my friend is than anything else could.

In its 30-plus years, Brennan's of Houston has survived floods, hurricanes, a tornado and small fires. We've been robbed. We've lost our air-conditioning more times than we like to remember, including once in August during a huge wedding reception. It hasn't been dull.

When Carl moved to Brennan's of Houston from Commander's Palace in September 1987, this city had been strangled by a serious economic downturn. Unemployment rates were almost on par with the humidity rate. Bankruptcies were common. Good restaurants closed.

Even though we tried some silly things, we weathered that challenge because we always understood that tradition matters. We are a restaurant based on tradition, not silly fads or IPO money. My family has been in the restaurant business for about a half-century. While we revere our heritage, we pride ourselves on never being fully satisfied, always innovating and staying passionate.

A Zagat Survey once noted, "Even New Orleans doesn't have a better New Orleans restaurant than Brennan's of Houston." That's the second nicest thing that's ever been said about this restaurant.

The first?

"We had a great time. We'll be back."

That's what Chef Carl Walker contributes to this restaurant. In this cookbook you will find passion and, oh yes, some world-class food as well.

Life is short; eat well!

— Alex Brennan-Martin

I express initial heartfelt thanks to God for my many families. My own: Rula, my wife of 21 years, my sons, Engel and Brandon, plus my parents, Louis and Gladys Walker, who raised me and nudged me in the right direction in life.

Two decades ago, I was blessed to cross paths with the Brennans, a stellar restaurant dynasty, who made me part of their family. I especially credit Ella Brennan, whose motto is "Pull no one up the mountain." Ella has never let me stop climbing. I'm eternally thankful for the opportunity to learn from countless Brennan family members, particularly Alex Brennan-Martin, my mentor and valued friend.

Early in 2000, anxiety and clinical depression gripped my life. Kay-La Hughes, my assistant, offered a lifeline with her friendship. A gifted doctor helped me understand depression doesn't mean an end or weakness, but a new beginning. Thus, I decided the time and team were ripe for our first cookbook, so that we might share our passion. Project coordinator Fran Fauntleroy kept me focused on that goal. I commend her experienced, positive guidance. We assembled a standout group of ardent individuals. Ellen Tipton, invaluable Director of Marketing, deciphered recipes, organized us, read my thoughts and put them in proper form. Sous Chefs Jose Arevalo, Randy Evans and Chris Shepherd reduced recipes from the quantities in our pot to your pot. They ran the kitchen flawlessly as I concentrated on the book. Our "Wine Guy," Martin Korson, aptly supported us with his expertise. The entire Brennan's team met our every need. I tip my chef's toque to our staff, past and present, for making

acknowledgments

Brennan's of Houston the exceptional restaurant it is. Laura Crucet, former Pastry Sous Chef, provided our preliminary recipe structure. Ann Steiner, diligent recipe editor, toiled day and night fine-tuning recipes. Artist Suzanne Morris, with pencils in hand, brought our art-filled cover to life. Barry Kilner translated Suzanne's art into the book's cover design. Mark Davis, photographer and Katie Dickie Stavinoha, editor, captured the true essence of Brennan's. I thank Rue Judd and the staff of Bright Sky Press, who worked with us to make this book "cook." I treasure the dedication of testers Mary Raybould, Sharon Hamilton and Georgia Shepherd, who prepared endless recipes in our "home" kitchen. We further extend our gratitude to Vernon Bartley, Judy Bell, Connie Castillo, Laura Crucet, Linda DeBolt, Michelle Helfman, Kay-La Hughes, Caroline Korson, Tracy Laman, Susan Middleton, Melissa Piper Reilly, Cindy Sloan, Sarah Swagerty, Ellen Tipton and Rula Walker for Creole recipe testing in their own kitchens.

Above-and-beyond-the-call-of-duty awards go to Shalom Shamooelian of Village Flowery, Francesca Nilsen and Pam Lopez of Distinctive Details, Nancy Griffin of Mani D'Oro, Melissa Piper Reilly of Sweets for the Occasion, Jay Rosenstein of Events and Rob and Melinda Emmons for providing Mardi Gras spirit all year long.

Most of all, Alex Brennan-Martin, the Brennan's of Houston staff, and I thank myriad friends and guests of the past 34 years, who have supplied the magic and memories that make our Creole hearts sing.

ix

F or my first interview with Ella Brennan, the famous New Orleans restaurateur who is legendary for businesses providing great food, great service, and great memories, I wore a three-piece suit. Needless to say, I was extremely nervous. She finally leaned over and said, "Relax or you're going to make me mad." Such comforting words.

I have deep respect and admiration for her, her family and the restaurants that I've become involved with as chef. She told me when she interviewed me, "You either run beside me or ahead of me. I pull no one — not even my own children — up the mountain."

Though Ella didn't know this during that first interview — I like challenges.

Like millions of others, when I was a 17-year-old farm boy, I struggled with the answer to "What do you want to do with your life?" I thought seeing the world would provide some perspective, so I joined the United States Marine Corps. My parents encouraged me to think about what I wanted to do when I left the Marines....Thankfully, I told the recruiter that I really liked to cook.

"Oh yeah, you can be a cook in the Marines. We'll even send you to school."

No way could I have predicted that declaration would continue to guide my career almost 30 years later. Nor could I have imagined I would one day offer fried oysters to former President George Bush, a

Crabmeat Ravigote and
Fried Green Tomatoes

introduction

Above: The Carl Walker U.S. Marine Corps Birthday Cake; Below: Maple syrup making on the family farm

Houston resident and a favorite guest at Brennan's of Houston, where I became chef in 1987.

Nonetheless, graduating at the top of my Marine Corps cooking class and serving up to 7,000 Marines per meal were the challenges that allowed me to really learn the food industry. More importantly, it revealed that cooking really was my special talent. It instilled confidence and motivated me to get serious about my passion for the skill and art of cooking and presentation. I continued my studies at the Culinary Institute of America.

I'm very lucky to love what I do and be involved with the Brennan family — a family that shares my enthusiasm for superb food, embraces the same hard work ethic, and continually pushes for excellence.

Despite my interview jitters, I got the job as a sous chef at Mr. B's in New Orleans. From there, I went over to Commander's Palace, and for four-and-a-half years I worked side-by-side with Chef Emeril Lagasse taking Commander's to new culinary heights. Then I answered the Brennan's challenge to do the same for Brennan's of Houston.

Striving for perfection in a restaurant that is known for its distinctive quality requires maintaining

a whirlwind pace day after day. I think growing up on a farm conditioned me for such a frenzy. Farmers don't have set hours, and they are very particular about what they produce — just like Brennan's of Houston.

On my family's Missouri farm, we always had a huge garden. My parents and grandparents were rarely satisfied with the vegetables they could buy at the local grocery store, which is probably why I'm on a never-ending search for fresh meats, cheeses, fruits and vegetables for the restaurant.

Our guests demand — and deserve no less than — the finest quality food and service. The restaurant has been in Houston for almost 35 years and is a revered institution for good times and special occasions. We try to make every meal a special memory — it's expected of all of us who work under the Brennan's of Houston umbrella.

We constantly strive to make good great and the best better. As I've learned from Ella and Alex Brennan-Martin, it's a religion. Today I have spectacular sous chefs who evangelize that work ethic and give that extra little something — *lagniappe* — that is truly a Brennan's specialty.

Above: Chef Carl with Julia Child, 1991; Below: Alex Brennan-Martin and Chef Carl, 2001

Our whole team — from the front to the back — has allowed

me the time to devote to this cookbook project because I want it to be a

cookbook that is used, not just a souvenir of Brennan's of Houston.

The true test of any cookbook is to find pages turned down

with splashes and splatters throughout.

At heart, I am a home cook. When I was 13, my mom took an

outside job, and cooking supper became my responsibility. Occasionally,

I would surprise my family with a candlelight dinner and a new recipe on

a night when my folks came home exhausted and hungry. My team and

I realize there are many nights when people head home tired, wanting to

duplicate meals with the quality they've come to expect at our restaurant.

We really thought about how to make things easiest for the everyday cook.

I recognize the need to make recipes that are useful and that don't scare people off with the number of ingredients or the perceived difficulty of preparation. I've included short-cuts like canned beef broth or the bouillon cube for intensifying flavor, as well as the longer process of making stocks from scratch. We get tremendous depth of flavor for our stock, which we prepare in great volume — 120 pounds of veal bones at a whack. So even if the home cook cannot exactly duplicate the intensity of the dishes we serve at Brennan's of Houston, we know these recipes work.

What's more, we spend a lot of time incorporating the little extras — from choosing a good wine to folding a linen napkin — that make a meal a dining experience. In this book, we include ideas and suggest ways you can use them in your own kitchen and dining room. We hope this book ends up stained and dog-eared as it inspires your own cooking and dining memories.

Left: Thomas Franklin with Smoked Chicken Salad ready for presentation

Though Brennan's of Houston lies 350 miles south and west of New Orleans, we certainly share the Big Easy's fondness for celebration — and all the necessary accompaniments for a proper festivity.

In our more than three decades in the Bayou City, we have hosted surprise engagements, elegant weddings, festive receptions, memorable christenings, numerous anniversaries, untold birthday parties, and who knows how many "deal-sealing" business lunches, dinners and brunches. No matter the occasion, from merry to mundane, we strive to make the beginning of the meal as memorable as the last — from the first, thirst-quenching drink to the appropriate wine with each course to the last sip of coffee. Our napkins even receive special attention — we'll pleat them or fold them into "birds of paradise" before inserting them into glasses. Or we'll tie them with special cording or bright ribbons and tuck in fresh herbs and flowers.

We've also developed a reputation for inventive, sumptuous appetizers — many with their foundation in Creole cuisine. One Easter, we nestled a jumbo shrimp which the chefs positioned to look like a rabbit, atop our favorite rice dish. We borrow the Cajun-Creole word *lagniappe*, which means a little something extra, to define our special offerings. For example, our Cajun Enchiladas started out as a *lagniappe*, but guests requested more, more, more; so today, the dish is available — and very popular — as a main course.

best of beginnings

Brennan's of Houston Mint Julep

## BRANDY MILK PUNCH MILKSHAKE

Yield: 4 servings

*Chef's Note: After sampling the ice cream version of a Brandy Milk Punch at Mr. B's Bistro in New Orleans, Mary Raybould, one of our very special guests, re-created this treat for us.*

1/2 cup brandy
2 tablespoons vanilla extract
1/4 cup milk
3 cups vanilla ice cream, slightly softened

Dash grated nutmeg

Place brandy, vanilla, milk and ice cream in blender; pulse until smooth.

Pour into 4 glasses and garnish with nutmeg.

Chef's Tip: To scoop ice cream more easily, microwave on 30-percent power in 30-second increments until softened. For the holidays, try eggnog ice cream instead of vanilla in this recipe.

*"Wine brings to light the hidden secrets of the soul."*

*— Horace*

18

Brandy Milk Punch Milkshake

Cosmopolitan Champagne Cocktail

## COSMOPOLITAN CHAMPAGNE COCKTAIL

Yield: 1 serving

*Chef's Notes: The pink hue of this cooling beverage lends itself well to spring and summer events, as well as for bridal showers and ladies' luncheons. Champagne aficionados find it irresistible.*

1 tablespoon Cointreau
2 tablespoons cranberry juice or
   cranberry juice cocktail
1/2 teaspoon Rose's lime juice or
   fresh lime juice
1 teaspoon Simple Syrup
   (recipe follows)
2 cups ice
Chilled champagne
1 twist of lemon

In a pitcher or shaker mix Cointreau, cranberry juice, lime juice and Simple Syrup together over ice to chill.

Strain Cointreau mixture into a champagne flute.

Top off glass with 4 to 5 ounces champagne. Garnish with a twist of lemon and serve.

## HURRICANE CARL

Yield: 4 servings

*Chef's Note: At first I thought this cocktail was named after me because the staff needed a drink after spending the day with me in the kitchen! Truth be told, this drink was concocted for our phenomenal Mardi Gras celebration since Hurricanes historically are the chosen beverage in New Orleans.*

2 tablespoons grenadine
1 teaspoon Simple Syrup
   (recipe follows)
Juice of 1 lime
Chilled champagne
4 thin lime slices for garnish

In a small pitcher make the base by stirring together grenadine, Simple Syrup and lime juice. Divide mixture evenly among 4 champagne flutes.

Top each glass off with 4 to 5 ounces champagne.

Garnish with a lime slice; cut and placed over edge of the glass.

## MARDI GRAS RITA

Yield: 1 serving

3 tablespoons tequila
1 tablespoon Cointreau
1 tablespoon Rose's lime juice
6 tablespoons sweet-and-sour mix
1 1/2 cups crushed ice
1 tablespoon Chambord
Lime wedge or cherry for garnish

Place tequila, Cointreau, lime juice, sweet-and-sour mix with ice in blender; process until slushy.

Pour half of mixture into glass. Pour Chambord over top of mixture in glass.

Pour remaining mixture into glass to complete layering; garnish with lime wedge or cherry.

Chef's Tips: This is a sweet margarita, so you can forego using salt on the rim!

Drop a shot of Grand Marnier into a regular frozen margarita for yet another sweet version of this traditional drink.

## SIMPLE SYRUP

1 cup water
1 cup sugar

Bring water and sugar to a simmer in a small saucepan over medium heat, about 1 to 2 minutes, or until sugar is dissolved. Chill and store in covered container in refrigerator to use as needed.

Mardi Gras Mambo Daiquiri

## MARDI GRAS MAMBO DAIQUIRI

Yield: 1 serving

4 tablespoons Southern Comfort whiskey
1 tablespoon Chambord
2 tablespoons cranberry juice or cranberry juice cocktail
2 tablespoons pineapple juice
1 1/2 cups ice
Maraschino cherry for garnish

Pour whiskey, Chambord, cranberry and pineapple juices with ice into a blender; process until slushy.

Pour into chilled glass and garnish with maraschino cherry.

Chef's Tip: If you prefer a slightly sweeter daiquiri, add 1 tablespoon powdered sugar to ingredients before processing in blender.

## MINT JULEP

Yield: 1 serving

*Chef's Note: The Mint Julep is a traditional Southern drink. At the restaurant we even have our own engraved julep cups. We wouldn't serve anything else at a Kentucky Derby Party held the first Saturday in May.*

20 leaves fresh mint
2 tablespoons Simple Syrup (page 19)
2 tablespoons hot water
Crushed ice
1/4 cup bourbon
Splash of lemon-lime soda
1 sprig fresh mint for garnish

Place mint leaves, Simple Syrup, and water in a 14-ounce mixing glass and muddle or mash to crush the leaves.

Fill silver tumbler with crushed ice. Strain mint mixture into tumbler and pour in bourbon and soda.

Stir drink until tumbler is frosty and garnish with mint sprig.

## SAZERAC COCKTAIL

Yield: 1 serving

*Chef's Note: Introduced at the Sazerac Bar in New Orleans' French Quarter, this is one of the most famous of New Orleans' drinks. If you're going there, pronounce it "SAZ-uh-rak."*

3 tablespoons rye whiskey or Kentucky bourbon
1 1/2 teaspoons powdered sugar
4 to 5 dashes Peychaud bitters
2 dashes Angostura bitters
1 cup ice
1 teaspoon Pernod
Lemon twist for garnish

Mix whiskey, sugar, Peychaud and Angostura bitters with ice in a mixing glass.

Coat inside of a martini glass with Pernod and pour out; strain whiskey mixture into glass.

Garnish with lemon twist.

Sazerac Cocktail

Martin Korson, award-winning "Wine Guy" at Brennan's of Houston

## MARTIN'S WINE THOUGHTS

I can't stand "wine worship;" it goes against everything I believe about hospitality. If the goal is to enjoy the wine and have a good time, then the last thing that we should do is promote outdated snobbery and the supposed rules that surround wine. In many restaurants, for some strange reason, customers are too often intimidated and made nervous about wine; that's not hospitality. There is only one rule; drink what you like, not what someone tells you to like.

Our goal is to make our guests comfortable with wine. We hope they will leave with a little more confidence having tried a wine and food pairing they may not have had on their own. That's why we've broken our list into categories of taste and body and discarded the old fashioned geographical listing. On our list you'll find great Bordeaux next to California Meritage wines next to some incredible Chilean Cabernets. It makes trying something new a little easier and a whole lot less intimidating!

## CAFÉ BRÛLOT

Yield: 6 servings

*Chef's Note: Mario and Marcelino Cantu, brothers who have been captains with the restaurant since its beginning, have sealed many "forever" memories with the magical presentation of this coffee. We serve it flaming in a special Brûlot bowl, which is a traditional wedding gift in New Orleans. In French, Brûlot means burnt brandy.*

1 cinnamon stick
10 whole cloves
1 orange, peeled into a spiral, about 12 inches
1 lemon, peeled into a spiral, about 3 to 4 inches
2½ tablespoons sugar
4 cups coffee (best made with chicory coffee)
¼ cup brandy
2 tablespoons Triple Sec

Break cinnamon stick into pieces and put it with cloves into a large tea infuser, or tie up in a small piece of cheesecloth. Set aside.

Heat orange and lemon spirals with sugar in a medium saucepan over low heat 1 minute. Add coffee and infuser with spices. Stir in brandy and Triple Sec; steep mixture on low heat 15 minutes.

Serve in demitasse cups with New Orleans-Style Pralines (page 168).

Chef's Tip: Always add coffee before stirring in brandy and Triple Sec. Although Café Brûlot is served as a flaming presentation at the restaurant, don't attempt this method at home unless you are experienced with the procedure.

23

Tableside Café Brûlot by Brothers Cantu

## LAGNIAPPE

We're always trying to inject lagniappe, the Cajun word for a little something extra, into our guests' dining experience. Ellen Tipton, our Director of Sales and Marketing, and our staff create many of our special effects.

At Brennan's of Houston, we use cookies in hundreds of shapes as place-cards, party favors, special messages, and lollipops to company logos, and in gift baskets. Our favorite cookie is shaped like a turtle — it's our symbol for entertaining and public relations. Children love them — just like they do ice cream cone-shaped cookies. We can match cookie colors to fabrics to complete an extra decorative touch. And we'll bake cookies on sticks to create a cookie bouquet that can be presented to guests as they depart.

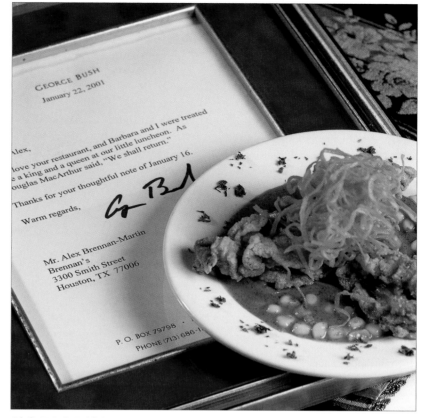

Chili-Fried Gulf Oysters

## CHILI-FRIED GULF OYSTERS

Yield: 6 servings

*Chef's Note: The masa-crusted oysters and colorful tequila-laced cream, pepper and corn sauce are a tempting favorite of former President George Bush, so we have the dish ready to go whenever he visits!*

3 cups Chili Corn Sauce
  (page 151)
Vegetable oil
3 cups very thin julienned sweet
  potatoes
3/4 cup cornmeal or "masa harina"
  corn flour

3/4 cup all-purpose flour
2 tablespoons Creole Seafood
  Seasoning, divided (page 157)
36 freshly shucked oysters

Prepare Chili Corn Sauce; reserve and keep warm.

Heat oil (2 inches deep) to 325 degrees in a deep fat fryer or a deep saucepan. If using a saucepan, refer to the Chef's Tip below. Fry sweet potatoes until crisp, drain on paper towels and reserve.

Combine cornmeal, flour and 1 tablespoon Creole Seafood Seasoning in a medium bowl. Season oysters with remaining 1 tablespoon Creole Seafood

Seasoning, dredge in flour mixture and fry in batches of 9 oysters at a time in same oil until crisp. Remove oysters and sprinkle with a little extra Creole Seafood Seasoning; drain on paper towels on a rack, keeping warm.

Ladle ½ cup Chili Corn Sauce in center of each plate. Place 6 oysters around edge of plate. Garnish with a mound of fried sweet potatoes in center of each plate.

Chef's Tips: Use a mandoline to cut sweet potatoes into very thin shoestrings. Whenever using a mandoline, be cautious not to cut yourself. For a shortcut, purchase sweet potato chips at the grocery.

When using dry spices such as chili powder, cumin, and cayenne, toast them slightly in a hot skillet over a low flame before using. Heat releases the oils and intensifies the flavor and character.

Fried shrimp are equally tempting for this dish. Home chefs may use this recipe as the base for another creation by preparing a filet mignon or fish fillet, saucing the filet, then arranging the oysters around the filet.

If you are using a saucepan on the stove for frying, be extremely careful to use one that can hold at least 2 inches of oil and still have 4 inches to the top edge of the saucepan. I also recommend using a thermometer if you are using the saucepan method.

## SPICED PECANS

Yield: 2 cups

2 cups pecans, pieces or halves
2 tablespoons Creole Seafood
   Seasoning (page 157)
2 tablespoons Louisiana
   hot pepper sauce
2 tablespoons Worcestershire sauce

Preheat oven to 250 degrees. In a medium bowl, mix pecans, Creole Seafood Seasoning, hot sauce and Worcestershire. Spread on a baking sheet and roast, stirring every 15 minutes, until dry and crispy, about 30 to 45 minutes. Cool to room temperature. Store in covered container.

Chef's Tip: Use pecan halves to create a spicy snack.

## GARLIC BREAD

Yield: 10 servings

*Chef's Note: For decades, Brennan's of Houston and Commander's Palace have made guests smile by offering a plate of hot and toasty garlic bread before their meal!*

1 fresh-baked French baguette
½ cup grated Parmesan cheese
2 tablespoons minced fresh garlic
1 teaspoon chopped fresh parsley
1 teaspoon salt
10 tablespoons unsalted butter,
   melted

Preheat oven to 450 degrees. Split loaf of bread lengthwise.

In a small bowl, blend cheese, garlic, parsley and salt; reserve. Brush cut sides of loaf with butter; sprinkle generously with reserved cheese mixture. Place bread on a baking sheet; bake 5 to 7 minutes, or until golden brown. Remove from oven; cut into desired size pieces.

Chef's Tip: Substitute 1 teaspoon garlic powder for fresh garlic.

25

Chef Carl and his collection

Cajun Enchiladas with Roasted Tomatillo Salsa

## CAJUN ENCHILADAS WITH ROASTED TOMATILLO SALSA

Yield: 4 appetizer servings

*Chef's Note: These spicy enchiladas napped in a lusty tomatillo sauce and garnished with sour cream guarantee oohs and aahs from gratified diners. This dish is a stunning appetizer with one enchilada or doubled for a special entrée. It is a true classic at Brennan's of Houston.*

2 cups Roasted Tomatillo Salsa
  (page 27)
1 cup Pico de Gallo
  (page 153)
3 tablespoons vegetable oil, divided
¼ cup finely chopped yellow onion
¼ cup finely chopped
  poblano pepper
¼ cup finely chopped
  red bell pepper
1 teaspoon minced garlic
1 pound cooked crawfish tail meat
1 tablespoon Louisiana hot
  pepper sauce
1 tablespoon Worcestershire sauce

1 cup shredded pepper Jack cheese,
  divided
Salt and black pepper to taste
4 corn tortillas
¼ cup sour cream
4 whole crawfish, boiled, for
  decoration (optional)

Prepare Roasted Tomatillo Salsa; reserve, keeping warm. Prepare Pico de Gallo; reserve.

Preheat oven to 400 degrees.

Heat 1 tablespoon oil in a medium skillet over medium-high heat. Add onion, poblano, bell pepper and garlic; sauté until onion is translucent.

Add crawfish, hot sauce and Worcestershire; heat through.

Add ½ cup cheese and heat until melted; season with salt and pepper.

In a separate small skillet, heat 2 tablespoons oil. Place tortillas quickly in and out of the hot oil to soften. Or, wrap tortillas in dampened paper towel and microwave on high 25 seconds to soften.

Divide crawfish mixture among tortillas, roll them up and place on an oiled sheet pan. Top with remaining ½ cup cheese and warm in oven about 7 minutes, or until hot.

Spoon ½ cup hot Roasted Tomatillo Salsa on each plate and place an enchilada directly from oven on salsa. Top with a dollop of sour cream and a sprinkle of reserved Pico de Gallo. Complete garnish with a whole, boiled crawfish. Or, place 1 cup salsa in a casserole, top with enchiladas and remaining ½ cup cheese; heat in oven until hot. Garnish as above; serve remaining 1 cup salsa on the side.

Chef's Tips: You can substitute shrimp, lobster or crab sautéed in vegetable oil and sprinkled with seafood spice. The most succulent crawfish are available from January to June from seafood markets or grocery stores in the South. If fresh crawfish are not available, you can find them frozen. When buying live crawfish, look for the ones that are lively and uniform in size. Our other enchilada fillings are duck confit, pheasant, smoked or roasted chicken — omitting the crawfish garnish.

## ROASTED TOMATILLO SALSA

Yield: 1 quart

*Chef's Note: Tomatillos are Mexican tomato-like fruit with a lemony flavor that are distinguished by their small size and thin, parchment-like covering. They are immensely popular in Southwestern cooking.*

3 cups tomatillos, cut into quarters
1½ cups cherry tomatoes, cut in half
¼ cup vegetable oil
¾ cup finely chopped onion
3 garlic cloves, very thinly sliced
1 jalapeño, seeded and minced
1 tablespoon ground cumin
¾ teaspoon dried oregano
2 cups chicken stock or canned chicken broth
Salt and black pepper to taste
1 tablespoon chopped fresh cilantro leaves

Preheat oven to 275 degrees.

Place tomatillos and tomatoes on sheet pan sprayed lightly with nonstick vegetable spray. Roast 30 to 60 minutes, or until semi-dry and beginning to caramelize.

Heat oil in a medium skillet over medium heat. Add onion and garlic; sauté 3 minutes, or until garlic starts to brown. Add roasted tomatillos, tomatoes, jalapeño, cumin, oregano and stock; bring to a simmer. Simmer 20 minutes, or until sauce is thickened. Season with salt and pepper. Sprinkle with cilantro just before serving.

Chef's Tips: Remember to remove the husks and wash the tomatillos before using.

This recipe is also a great sauce for roasted meat dishes such as chicken, veal or pork.

I could see a nice grilled pork tenderloin finished with this salsa and served with the Texas Cornbread Pudding (page 143).

27

## CRAWFISH PIE

Yield: 4 servings

2 tablespoons vegetable oil
1/2 cup finely chopped poblano
   pepper
1/2 cup finely chopped red bell
   pepper
1/2 cup finely chopped yellow onion
1 pound crawfish tail meat
1/2 teaspoon cumin
2 teaspoons Creole Seafood
   Seasoning (page 157)
2 tablespoons Louisiana hot
   pepper sauce
2 tablespoons Worcestershire sauce
1 cup grated pepper Jack cheese
1/2 recipe Dad's Hush Puppies
   batter (page 147)
4 teaspoons salted butter

Heat oil in a medium skillet over medium heat; add poblano and red peppers and onion. Sauté until vegetables are translucent. Add crawfish and cook until crawfish are hot. Mix in cumin, Creole Seafood Seasoning, hot sauce and Worcestershire.

Remove skillet from heat. Fold in cheese and allow cheese to melt. Divide ingredients evenly among 4 (5-inch) ungreased skillets or ovenproof ramekins.

Preheat oven to 350 degrees. Prepare Hush Puppies batter and evenly cover crawfish mixture in skillets.

Bake 15 minutes, or until batter is cooked through when a toothpick inserted in center of batter comes out clean Remove from oven and top each serving with 1 teaspoon butter. Dust handles of the skillets with a little flour to symbolize "hot" handles. Serve piping hot.

Chef's Tip: The miniature skillet or ramekin presentation is a great one for guests to see; however, if you don't have 5-inch skillets or ramekins, consider making this recipe in one large skillet. Top with Dad's Hush Puppies batter, allowing a longer cooking time. Check for doneness by inserting a toothpick into the center as described in the recipe. It's fun to see the smiles when the steaming skillet arrives tableside for serving! Small skillets are available at kitchenware stores.

## CARAMELIZED ONION AND PARMESAN TARTLETS

Yield: 4 dozen

*Chef's Note: Talk about quick, easy and a boon for vegetarians!*

1 tablespoon vegetable oil
1 large yellow onion, cut into
   1/2-inch julienne strips
1 egg
1/2 cup whipping cream
1/3 cup finely grated Parmesan
   cheese
1/2 teaspoon finely chopped
   fresh basil
1/2 teaspoon finely chopped
   fresh thyme
1/2 teaspoon finely chopped
   fresh oregano
Salt and black pepper to taste
48 (1 1/2 wide x 3/4 inch)
   mini tartlet shells, pre-baked
Sour cream for garnish (optional)
Finely chopped fresh chives for
   garnish (optional)

Heat oil in a medium skillet over medium to medium-high heat; add onion. Stirring every minute, sauté onion 6 to 8 minutes or until onion is caramelized to a nice golden brown. Remove from heat, cool and reserve.

In a medium mixing bowl, whisk egg slightly. Add cream, cheese, basil, thyme, oregano and reserved onion. Season custard mixture with salt and pepper. At this point you may cover and refrigerate custard until closer to party time that day.

Preheat oven to 350 degrees. When ready to bake, fill shells almost to the rim with custard, being careful to have an equal amount of onion in each cup. Bake 12 to 15 minutes, or until custard is set. Serve warm.

To garnish, combine sour cream and chives in a small bowl. Crown each tartlet with a small dollop of the herbed sour cream.

Chef's Tips: Tartlet shells are usually available at grocery stores or gourmet shops. If you can't find the shells, layer 4 sheets of phyllo dough, brushing each sheet with melted, unsalted butter. Cut circles or squares to fit a mini muffin pan. Pre-bake the phyllo cups at 325 degrees 5 minutes, or until they start to brown. Fill with custard and bake until custard is set.

Other fillings you might want to use include our Creamed Spinach (page 75) for another vegetarian version, or our Cajun Enchilada filling (page 26) topped with Pico de Gallo (page 153). If you choose the crawfish filling, dice the crawfish a little more. With so many options, you can just let your imagination run wild!

Crawfish Pie

## CLASSIC SHRIMP REMOULADE

Yield: 6 servings

*Chef's Note: Shrimp Remoulade is a true New Orleans classic. Many variations exist, but I believe the ultimate is when the freshly cooked, warm shrimp are mixed with cold Remoulade Sauce. The sauce pairs well with other seafood, such as tossing with crabmeat or drizzling over fried catfish.*

1 1/2 cups Remoulade Sauce (recipe follows)
Simple Vinaigrette Dressing (recipe follows)
1 1/2 pounds (26/30 or 36/42 count) shrimp
Shrimp Boil (page 156)
1 1/2 cups very thinly sliced cucumbers, seeds removed but not peeled
1/2 cup very thinly sliced radishes
2 cups frisée or curly endive

Prepare Remoulade Sauce; refrigerate until needed. Prepare Simple Vinaigrette Dressing; reserve until needed. Peel and devein shrimp; reserve.

Prepare Shrimp Boil; add shrimp and simmer 1 to 2 minutes, or until shrimp are cooked through. Strain shrimp from Shrimp Boil. In a medium bowl, toss shrimp in reserved Remoulade Sauce to thoroughly coat; set aside.

In a separate medium bowl, toss cucumbers, radishes and frisee in reserved Simple Vinaigrette Dressing. Evenly divide cucumber, radish and frisée mixture and place in center of each plate.

Arrange shrimp on top of salad.

Chef's Tips: It's best to use the size of shrimp we recommend for this recipe. However, the way you cook the shrimp is most important.

## REMOULADE SAUCE

Yield: 2 1/2 cups

1/4 cup ketchup
1/4 cup prepared horseradish
1/4 cup Creole mustard, such as Zatarain's
2 tablespoons prepared yellow mustard
2 tablespoons white vinegar
Juice of 1/2 lemon
1/2 cup finely chopped green onion
1/4 cup finely chopped celery
1/4 cup finely chopped parsley
1 garlic clove, minced
1 tablespoon paprika
1/8 teaspoon cayenne pepper
1/4 teaspoon salt
Dash Tabasco
1 fresh egg or pasteurized equivalent
3/4 cup vegetable oil

Put ketchup, horseradish, Creole and prepared mustards, vinegar, lemon juice, onion, celery, parsley, garlic, paprika, pepper, salt, Tabasco and egg into blender container or food processor. Cover and mix at high speed until well blended. Remove cover and gradually add oil in a slow steady stream. Sauce will thicken to a pourable, creamy consistency.

Store in covered container in refrigerator up to 3 days.

Chef's Tips: If concerned about using raw eggs in this recipe, substitute an equivalent pasteurized egg product according to manufacturer's instructions.

One of my favorite ways to use Remoulade Sauce is to warm up some crawfish tail meat and season it with a sprinkle of Creole Seafood Seasoning to serve Crawfish Remoulade.

## SIMPLE VINAIGRETTE DRESSING

1/2 cup red wine vinegar
1 tablespoon pickling spices
1 tablespoon sugar
1/2 tablespoon vegetable oil

Place vinegar, pickling spices, sugar and oil in a small saucepan. Bring to a boil over medium-high heat. Lower heat and simmer 5 minutes, or until liquid is reduced by half. Strain and store in covered container in refrigerator until needed.

*"I never eat when I can dine."*
*— Maurice Chevalier*

Classic Shrimp Remoulade

31

## CHICKEN EMPANADITAS

Yield: 4 dozen

*Chef's Note: Holiday time or any time, this hors d'oeuvre is one that is in constant demand. Our empanaditas are small, filled, savory turnovers.*

8 ounces boneless, skinless chicken breast or thigh
Creole Meat Seasoning (page 156)
1 tablespoon vegetable oil
1/2 cup finely chopped red bell pepper
1/4 cup finely chopped poblano pepper
1/4 cup finely chopped red onion
1 tablespoon Louisiana hot pepper sauce
1 tablespoon Worcestershire sauce
1/2 cup shredded pepper Jack cheese
Fresh pasta sheets or egg roll wrappers, amount varies depending on size of pasta sheets and quantity in packages of wrappers
1 egg
1 tablespoon water
All-purpose flour as needed
1 cup Creole Mustard Cream Sauce for dipping (recipe follows)

Preheat oven to 350 degrees. Season chicken with 1 teaspoon Creole Meat Seasoning and roast 20 to 25 minutes, or until completely cooked through. Or, grill chicken. Cool chicken slightly, then chop finely; reserve.

Heat oil in a medium skillet over medium heat; sauté red and poblano peppers with onion 1 to 2 minutes, or until onion starts to become transparent. Add reserved chicken, hot sauce and Worcestershire. Sauté until hot.

Remove from heat, fold in cheese and adjust seasoning with additional meat seasoning, if needed; reserve.

Cut 2 1/2-inch circles in pasta sheets or eggroll wrappers with a round cookie cutter. Combine egg and water in a small bowl. Brush pasta or eggroll circle around the edges with egg wash. Place 1 heaping teaspoon reserved chicken filling in center of each circle. Fold each circle in half and crimp edges together using a fork dipped in a small dish of flour. Re-dip fork in flour when fork gets sticky.

At this point the empanaditas may be placed on wax paper on a sheet pan or wrapped in plastic wrap and frozen until time to use. They will keep up to 1 month in the freezer. If empanaditas are frozen, thaw slightly in refrigerator before cooking.

When ready to cook empanaditas, prepare Creole Mustard Cream Sauce; reserve.

Preheat oil in a deep fryer to 325 degrees. In batches fry empanaditas, 2 to 3 minutes, or until they begin to float and become golden. Remove and place on paper towels to drain. Keep warm until all empanaditas are fried. Serve immediately with reserved Creole Mustard Cream Sauce.

Chef's Tip: Cooked crawfish, shrimp and crabmeat are appetizing alternatives for the chicken in the empanadita filling.

## CREOLE MUSTARD CREAM SAUCE

Yield: 1 cup

3/4 cup whipping cream
1/4 cup Creole mustard or whole grain mustard
Salt and black pepper to taste

In a small saucepan over medium heat, cook cream about 10 minutes, or until slightly reduced and somewhat thickened. Whisk in mustard until fully blended. Season with salt and pepper. Serve warm as a dipping sauce in a small bowl.

Chef's Tips: If you can't find Creole Mustard, substitute whole-grain mustard. This easy-to-make sauce goes well with chicken, veal or pork. When using the sauce for meat, I like to add a couple of tablespoons of demi-glacé to boost the meat flavor.

## JOSE'S SHRIMP & TASSO EN BROCHETTE

Yield: 10 servings

*Chef's Note: Jose Arevalo has been at Brennan's of Houston for 19 years. As the Creole chef in our kitchen, he is the expert who understands Creole cooking and is our kitchen's "taste master." To create this hors d'oeuvre, Jose took an already great shrimp appetizer and enhanced it by wrapping the stuffed shrimp with tasso ham.*

Jose's Shrimp & Tasso En Brochette

20 (26/30 count) shrimp, tail on, peeled and deveined

1 jalapeño pepper, cut lengthwise, seeded and cut into thin slivers

1/4 yellow onion, cut into thin julienne strips 1 1/4-inches long

2 ounces pepper Jack cheese, cut into 1/4 x 1/4 x1-inch pieces

4 ounces tasso ham or Cajun-spiced ham, thinly sliced

Vegetable oil for deep frying

1 cup all-purpose flour

2 tablespoons Creole Seafood Seasoning, divided (page 157)

1/2 cup milk

1 egg

1 recipe Hot Sauce Beurre Blanc (page 155)

Butterfly the shrimp by cutting from head to tail along the center vein with a small knife. Lay shrimp out flat. Place a sliver of jalapeño, onion, and piece of cheese lengthwise on one cut side of each shrimp.

Close shrimp; wrap a slice of tasso around shrimp to hold in the goodies. Wrap tasso around shrimp twice if it looks too thin. Secure with a toothpick. Preheat oil in deep fryer to 325 degrees.

Combine flour with 1 tablespoon seafood seasoning in a small bowl. Mix milk and egg in another small bowl. Sprinkle shrimp with remaining 1 tablespoon seasoning.

Prepare Hot Sauce Beurre Blanc; reserve and keep warm.

Dip shrimp into egg wash and then dip into flour mixture. Fry shrimp in deep fryer until golden brown, about 2 to 3 minutes.

Shrimp will start to float to the top when done. Remove shrimp from oil and drain on paper towels.

Pair shrimp with reserved warm Hot Sauce Beurre Blanc for dipping.

**Chef's Tips: Instead of toothpicks, we use 6-inch bamboo skewers for the shrimp to create a dramatic look and to provide our guests with a nice handle to dip into the sauce. We served this appetizer at the James Beard House in 1998 with the Texas Beef Council along with the winner of the Texas Beef Cook-Off. For a new twist, we used rosemary skewers and roasted the shrimp.**

## CREOLE BARBECUE SHRIMP

Yield: 4 servings

*Chef's Note: I was Emeril Lagasse's sous chef at Commander's Palace for four-and-a-half years. Following a meal at his own restaurant, Emeril's, in New Orleans, I developed the Louisiana barbecue base for this popular jumbo shrimp dish. As a contrast, I also concocted a Texas Cornbread Pudding (page 143) that has a jalapeño bite, and a refreshing Jicama Slaw (page 35) to accompany the shrimp.*

³/₄ cup Barbecue Sauce Base (page 35)
¹/₂ teaspoon vegetable oil
¹/₃ cup julienned red bell pepper
¹/₃ cup julienned poblano pepper
¹/₃ cup sliced yellow onion
³/₄ teaspoon minced garlic
20 (16/20 per pound) headless shrimp, peeled and cleaned — sprinkled with a little Creole Seafood Seasoning (page 157)
¹/₄ cup whipping cream

Prepare Barbecue Sauce Base; reserve, keeping warm.

Heat oil in a large skillet over medium heat. Add red and poblano peppers, onion and garlic; sauté about 40 seconds. Add shrimp and sauté 30 seconds. Stir in Barbecue Sauce Base.

Add cream and simmer 2 to 3 minutes, or until shrimp are cooked. If the sauce seems a little too spicy, add a little cream to tone it down.

Chef's Tips: We peel our jumbo shrimp, leaving the tail intact. Then we butterfly and devein each shrimp before sautéing it.

We make this recipe with sautéed oysters in place of the shrimp and serve over a nice fillet of grilled fish.

Creole Barbecue Shrimp

## BARBECUE SAUCE BASE

Yield: 4 servings or about 1 cup

2½ lemons, peeled and quartered
3 tablespoons coarse-ground
   black pepper
2 tablespoons Creole Seafood
   Seasoning (page 157)
1 cup Worcestershire sauce
1 cup water or shrimp stock
5 garlic cloves

In a medium saucepan, combine lemons, pepper, Creole Seafood Seasoning, Worcestershire, water and garlic. Simmer uncovered until liquid is reduced by half. Strain through a fine-mesh strainer and reserve liquid. Store in covered container in refrigerator up to 2 weeks.

## JICAMA SLAW

Yield: 1½ cups

*Chef's Note: Jicama is a tropical root vegetable found in markets throughout Mexico and the American Southwest. Its brown outer skin hides a crunchy white flesh that is intensely refreshing during hot weather or when combined with our spicy Creole Barbecue Shrimp (page 34).*

1½ cups peeled and
   julienned jicama
Juice of 1 lime
Salt and freshly ground black
   pepper to taste

Place jicama in a small bowl. Season jicama with lime juice, salt and pepper.

## SMOKED SALMON PIZZA WITH CHÈVRE

Yield: 8 appetizer servings

*Chef's Note: Everyone loves pizza — especially my teen-age sons. There are several quick ways to make the crust: Buy a pre-made crust at the grocery or use a crust mix that you can make in about 15 minutes. Just be sure to pre-bake the crust before adding the toppings.*

1 tablespoon virgin olive oil
1 (10-inch) thin pizza crust,
   pre-baked
4 ounces Scottish smoked salmon,
   thinly sliced
¼ cup crumbled chèvre
2 tablespoons finely chopped
   red onion
1 tablespoon chopped fresh dill
1 tablespoon chopped capers

Preheat oven to 375 degrees.
   Spread oil evenly on pizza crust; arrange salmon over crust. Sprinkle cheese over pizza, followed by onion, dill and capers.
   Bake on baking sheet until pizza starts to turn golden around edges, about 5 minutes. Cut into wedges.

**Chef's Tips:** I love Scottish smoked salmon (see the Source Guide, page 186) but there are other interesting ingredients you can use to make the pizzas. For example, Shrimp Remoulade Pizza — put a thin layer of Remoulade Sauce (page 31) on a pre-baked crust, top with a thin layer of chiffonade of lettuce, followed by a generous portion of small cooked shrimp. Drizzle with Remoulade Sauce and serve cold.

Or use seafood filling for the Cajun Enchiladas and the Roasted Tomatillo Salsa (page 27) to create another unique pizza appetizer. Brush a layer of the salsa over the pre-baked crust and top with the enchilada filling; sprinkle with pepper Jack cheese to complete before baking.

36

Smoked Salmon Cheesecake

## SMOKED SALMON CHEESECAKE

Yield: 1 (10-inch) cheesecake
12 servings

*Chef's Note: For its infinite variety of presentations, this recipe is a creative classic. It runs the gamut from hors d'oeuvres to luncheon salad to dinner entrée.*

2 cups crumbled Homestyle
   Cornbread (page 145)
1/4 cup unsalted butter, melted
4 1/2 (8-ounce) packages cream
   cheese, softened
1/2 cup sour cream
7 eggs
1/2 teaspoon salt
1/2 teaspoon white pepper
8 ounces smoked salmon
1 tablespoon paprika
1 1/2 pounds goat cheese, softened
3 tablespoons chopped fresh dill
1/2 recipe Creamy Dill Dressing
   (page 54)
1/3 cup finely diced red onion
1/3 cup finely chopped hard cooked
   egg whites
1/3 cup finely chopped hard cooked
   egg yolks
1/3 cup finely chopped capers

Prepare Homestyle Cornbread; reserve until needed.

Preheat oven to 325 degrees. In a medium bowl, combine cornbread and butter. Press mixture into bottom of a buttered and floured 10-inch spring-form pan; set aside.

In a large bowl using a hand mixer, beat cream cheese and sour cream until soft and fluffy; scrape down sides. Add eggs, one at a time, scraping down bowl after each addition. Blend in salt and pepper, then divide mixture equally into two medium mixing bowls. In bowl of food processor, purée salmon until smooth.

Add salmon purée and paprika to one of the bowls of cream cheese mixture; mix well. Add goat cheese and dill to other bowl of cream cheese mixture; mix well. Evenly pour goat cheese/ cream cheese mixture on top of cornbread. Evenly pour salmon/cream cheese mixture on top of goat cheese/cream cheese mixture.

Set springform pan on an 18-inch square of heavy-duty aluminum foil; crimp foil up sides of pan to prevent any moisture from seeping into crust. Bake in a water bath 60 minutes, or until cheesecake feels firm in the center. Cool to room temperature, then refrigerate until thoroughly chilled or freeze before cutting with a hot, clean serrated knife.

Prepare Creamy Dill Dressing; reserve until needed.

This cheesecake is best served lightly warmed. Place individual portion on a microwave-safe plate; heat 1 minute on 70-percent power. For presentation, sprinkle each serving plate with 1 teaspoon each of red onion, egg white, yolk and capers. Transfer warm slice of cheesecake onto plate and drizzle with Creamy Dill Dressing.

Chef's Tips:  Have fun with any of the following variations: Layer 4 sheets, each lightly buttered, of phyllo dough. Cut 4 to 5-inch squares of phyllo and press down into regular size muffin tins coated with vegetable spray. Press squares of aluminum foil down on top of the phyllo and place a few dried beans or pie weights on top. Pre-bake phyllo lightly, about 3 to 5 minutes at 325 degrees. Remove foil and weights but leave phyllo cups in tins. Fill cups with the two layers of cheesecake filling and bake until filling is set, about 15 to 20 minutes. Top each cheesecake with thinly sliced smoked salmon, rolled up into a rosette. Serve with a salad of baby greens tossed with dill dressing for a first course or light luncheon entrée. Traditional garnishes of red onion, egg whites, yolks and capers can be added to the plate.

For hors d'oeuvres, cut smaller squares of phyllo and press into miniature muffin tins, following the same procedure as above. However, shorten cooking time when filled.

## PROUDLY TEXAN

At first, Brennan's of Houston was a New Orleans restaurant in Texas — a successful copy. As we matured, our Houston team — dedicated to fine food and hospitality — began to influence menus.

Chilies and salsas crept into dishes. A unique style grew with its own distinct personality. Never denying our Creole roots, we prevailed upon the local bounty until one day we were no longer a New Orleans-style restaurant in Texas.

Today, we are proudly Texan, fiercely loyal to Houston customs and a Texas Creole restaurant — befitting the distinct, regional influences from which we drew.

## PAN-SEARED FOIE GRAS

Yield: 4 servings

*Chef's Notes: This appetizer is a very simple, tasty dish created by Sous Chef Chris Shepherd. Foie gras means fat liver in French; its use originated in ancient Egypt. Foie gras may be either goose or duck liver. Duck liver is the more widely produced in the U.S. We also use foie gras in pâtés and terrines. It's a power-packed accompaniment to a number of dishes enriching their flavor with its fullness and silkiness.*

¼ cup Veal or Beef demi-glacé (optional but worth it!), (page 69)
½ cup Spiced Pecans (page 25)
12 ounces foie gras
Pinch salt and black pepper
1 ½ cups julienned Granny Smith apple
2 tablespoons praline liqueur
2 cups baby frisée (or julienned chicory or Belgian endive)

Prepare Veal demi-glacé; reserve, keeping warm. Prepare Spiced Pecans, reserve until needed. Slice foie gras on a bias ½ to ¾-inch thick, into about 3-ounce portions. Season on both sides with salt and pepper.

In a medium skillet over high heat, sear foie gras 1 minute; turn and sear on the other side 30 seconds. When searing foie gras, warm it all the way through. Remove foie gras from skillet and keep warm.

Add apple to same skillet and sauté about 1 minute, or until apple starts to caramelize. There will be enough fat rendered from the foie gras to sauté the apple. Deglaze skillet with praline liqueur Add frisée to skillet and wilt slightly; toss in reserved pecans. Remove from heat.

Divide apple mixture evenly among 4 plates. Top each with a piece of reserved foie gras. Drizzle reserved demi-glacé over and around the plate. Serve immediately.

Chef's Tips: Foie gras is quite expensive. It is offered in A, B or C grades, with A being the best. Check gourmet food stores or our Source Guide.

You may substitute chicken livers for the foie gras. Be sure to sauté until done all the way through.

*"A bottle of wine begs to be shared. I have never met a miserly wine lover."*
*— Clifton Fadiman*

Sous Chefs Randy and José (seated) and Chris (standing) with Chef Carl

**W**e've always invited people to come into our kitchen. No dishwasher or food prep person bats an eye when an entourage walks through. Several years ago, we set up our own Kitchen Table…diners sit there, have their meal and talk with the chefs about the various dishes. It's a huge hit — people even give "Kitchen Table" dinners as a special gift — it sometimes takes several months to get a weekend reservation.

It won't take long for "kitchen" guests to learn that Turtle Soup is the most-requested item on our menu. We use the turtle as Brennan's of Houston's own symbol.

Staying true to our Creole customs and taking advantage of local fresh produce and seafood, we've tweaked and invented and let our imagination guide us in teaming seafood with crisp greens to satisfy the most discerning tastes. Hot, cold, crunchy, crisp — all satisfying in their manner to start a meal or to serve as the main course. A much-loved Crabmeat Ravigote with Fried Green Tomatoes marries all those sensations — with each bite a surprise as the textures change and blend. As a child and an adult, I was never fond of parsnips. However, this dish, with its slender strips of fried parsnips piled atop the mixed greens, will change the mind of any reluctant parsnip eater. It did mine.

from the garden and beyond

Asparagus Crab Vichyssoise

Creole Caesar Shrimp Salad

## CREOLE CAESAR SHRIMP SALAD

Yield: 4 large servings

*Chef's Note: This salad earned "Most Creative" at Houston's annual Caesar Salad competition in 1998. We served it with a mini Hurricane Carl drink (page 19) to capture the Creole spirit.*

1 cup Spicy Caesar Dressing (page 43)
Oil for deep frying
1 medium sweet potato, peeled
1 pound (16/20 count) shrimp, peeled and cleaned
1 tablespoon Creole Seafood Seasoning (page 157)
1/2 cup all-purpose flour
1/2 cup cornmeal
2 teaspoons Creole Seafood Seasoning
1 egg
1/2 cup milk
6 cups torn romaine hearts

1 cup torn radicchio
1/2 cup shaved Parmigiano-Reggiano cheese
1/2 cup thinly sliced tasso ham or Cajun-spiced deli ham

Prepare Spicy Caesar Dressing; reserve until needed. Heat oil in deep fryer to 325 degrees.

Slice potato as thinly as possible, preferably less than 1/8-inch. Fry slices in hot oil until potato chips are crisp. Place slices on a paper towel to drain; reserve.

Season shrimp with 1 table-spoon Creole Seafood Seasoning. Combine flour, cornmeal and 2 teaspoons Creole Seafood Seasoning in small bowl. Lightly dust shrimp with flour mixture.

Combine egg and milk in a small bowl and dip shrimp into egg wash. Dip shrimp back into flour mixture. Fry shrimp in hot oil about 2 minutes. Remove and drain on paper towel..

Toss romaine, radicchio, Parmigiano and tasso in a large bowl with reserved Spicy Caesar Dressing. Divide salad evenly among four plates and garnish with fried shrimp and sweet potato chips.

Chef's Tips: Tasso is a highly seasoned cured pork that is smoked and fully cooked.

To save time, use store-bought sweet potato chips.

Make this salad even better by using Jose's Shrimp & Tasso En Brochette (page 33) in this recipe. Dip the shrimp in Hot Sauce Beurre Blanc (page 155). It's like having "hot wing shrimp."

## SPICY CAESAR DRESSING

Yield: 1 cup

1 tablespoon fresh lemon juice
1 egg yolk or pasteurized equivalent
6 tablespoons grated Parmesan cheese
1 tablespoon minced garlic
1/2 tablespoon Worcestershire sauce
1 tablespoon red wine vinegar
1 tablespoon Dijon mustard
1 minced anchovy filet
2/3 cup vegetable oil
1/2 tablespoon Tabasco sauce
1/8 teaspoon red pepper flakes
1/4 teaspoon salt

Place lemon juice, egg yolk, Parmesan, garlic, Worcestershire, vinegar, mustard and anchovy in food processor or blender. Pulse ingredients a few times to blend. Slowly add oil to mixture while blending. When all of oil is incorporated, add Tabasco sauce, pepper flakes and salt; blend.

Store in covered container in refrigerator up to 3 days.

## JACKSON SALAD

Yield: 4 servings

*Chef's Note: This salad was the original Brennan's of Houston house salad. Even when we take it off the menu for a while, guests order as if it's still on the menu. Some guests request a Jill Jackson Salad, named for Ella Brennan's best friend. That's when we shower 1/4 cup crumbled blue cheese over the top to gild the lily!*

1/2 cup Jackson Dressing (recipe follows)
8 cups loosely packed mixed salad greens, washed and dried
1 hard-cooked egg, finely chopped
5 slices bacon, cooked until crisp, chopped

Prepare Jackson Dressing; reserve. In a large bowl, toss salad greens with dressing.

Divide greens evenly among 4 salad plates. Sprinkle egg and bacon over greens.

## JACKSON DRESSING

Yield: 1 1/2 cups

1 egg yolk or pasteurized equivalent
4 tablespoons Dijon mustard
2 tablespoons minced yellow onion
2 tablespoons red wine vinegar
1/2 teaspoon salt
1 cup vegetable oil
2 teaspoons freshly ground black pepper

In a blender or food processor, combine egg yolk, mustard, onion, vinegar and salt.

With motor running, very slowly pour oil into blender or food processor until oil is com-pletely incorporated.

Season with pepper and addi-tional salt if needed; mix well.

Store in covered container in refrigerator up to 3 days.

## Mama's Famous Spinach Salad

Yield : 4 servings

*Chef's Note:  Salad lovers look no further! This is one for the "Salad Hall of Fame." Its creator was Florence Gibson, better known as Mama. This salad has been enjoyed for years and the bacon dressing and deviled eggs she served with it were second to none. We were blessed to have Mama with us 33 years. During that time, Florence launched the careers of countless men and women who aspired to be chefs. Although we lost Mama in 2000 to the great kitchen in the sky, her wonderful salads and carrot cake live on.*

3/4 cup Mama's Bacon Dressing
    (recipe follows)
1 tablespoon vegetable oil
1 large onion, sliced
1/4 cup packed brown sugar
1/4 cup apple cider vinegar
6 cups fresh spinach, stemmed
12 mushroom caps, thinly sliced
2 ripe medium Roma tomatoes,
    cut into wedges
4 hard-cooked eggs, chopped

Prepare Mama's Bacon Dressing. Heat oil in a medium skillet over low heat; add onion and cook 10 to 15 minutes, or until caramelized.

Add sugar and vinegar; cook until reduced to a syrupy consistency, about 10 to 15 minutes. Reserve refrigerated until ready to use.

Thoroughly wash spinach in cold water; pat dry. In a large bowl, toss spinach, mushrooms and reserved bacon dressing. Divide dressed spinach among plates; garnish with tomato wedges, egg and reserved candied onion.

Chef's Tips:  Instead of garnishing this salad with chopped egg, embellish with deviled eggs.

For my own use, I double the candied onion — and pile it on my sandwiches.

## Mama's Bacon Dressing

Yield: 3 1/2 cups

*Chef's Note: This dressing is what puts Mama's Famous Spinach Salad over the top!*

12 ounces bacon
1/2 cup chopped onion
3/4 cup prepared yellow mustard
1/2 cup packed brown sugar
1 tablespoon minced garlic
2 cups vegetable oil
1/4 cup red wine vinegar
1 teaspoon dry mustard powder
1 teaspoon finely ground
    black pepper
1 teaspoon dried oregano leaves
Salt to taste

In a large skillet over medium-high heat, render bacon until crispy. Place bacon on paper towel to absorb extra fat. Coarsely chop bacon and set aside. Drain fat from skillet. Add onion to skillet and sauté until translucent; lower heat, and add prepared mustard, sugar and garlic. Simmer 2 to 3 minutes.

Transfer mixture from skillet to blender; add bacon pieces and purée until smooth. Place mixture in a large bowl and refrigerate until cool, about 20 minutes.

Measure oil and vinegar into a 4-cup glass measure. Whisk in dry mustard powder, pepper, oregano and salt. Slowly whisk oil mixture into bacon mixture until thoroughly combined.

Store in covered container in refrigerator up to 2 weeks.

Mama's Famous Spinach Salad

46

Sachnowitz Salad

## SACHNOWITZ SALAD

Yield: 4 servings

*Chef's Note: This salad was created by Larry Sachnowitz, a very dear friend and neighbor of the restaurant. We honor his spirit with this tribute to his skill with everything from the garden. Belgian endive and grapefruit sections are brought together with a citrus and mint vinaigrette — a wonderful combination of ingredients that complement each other.*

### BELGIAN ENDIVE

Belgian endive is about 6 inches long and creamy colored with yellow-edged leaves. This endive is slightly bitter and grown in total darkness. Always store in darkness — light increases bitterness.

Belgian endive is also an excellent vegetable to braise in a good chicken stock until tender; remove and finish as a gratinée with a little freshly grated Parmesan cheese and browned butter.

### HOW TO SEGMENT CITRUS

To segment an orange or grapefruit, place fruit on a cutting board and use a small sharp paring knife to cut off each end of citrus down to the fruit. Set fruit on cut end and cut just deep enough to remove the white surface down to the fruit. Once peeled, place fruit on side and cut on each side of segment membrane, staying as close to the membrane as possible, which will yield nice citrus wedges.

---

1 cup Citrus Mint Dressing (recipe follows)
6 medium Belgian endive
2 grapefruit, segmented (see directions)
1 tablespoon chiffonade mint leaves

Prepare Citrus Mint Dressing; reserve until needed. Remove 12 large leaves from endive and reserve. Chiffonade remaining endive crosswise into 1/4-inch pieces; set aside. Reserve 12 grapefruit sections; dice remaining grapefruit.

In a large bowl, toss diced grapefruit and chiffonade endive in Citrus Mint Dressing. To serve, place 3 endive leaves pointed up and out on each plate and top with dressed salad; garnish with reserved grapefruit sections and mint chiffonade.

Chef's Tips: An attractive presentation is to chiffonade an ingredient, which means to slice into strips varying from very thin to 1/4-inch.

If desired, Boston lettuce can be included with this recipe. Reserve 4 leaves and tear lettuce to yield 2 cups. Add torn lettuce to diced grapefruit and endive chiffonade; toss with reserved dressing. Place a Boston leaf on each plate, then 3 endive leaves pointed up and out and top with the dressed endive mixture. Garnish as described.

---

## CITRUS MINT DRESSING

Yield: 2 1/2 cups

1 grapefruit, sectioned
1 orange, sectioned
1 large shallot, thinly sliced
1/2 cup rice wine vinegar
1/4 cup olive oil
1/4 cup vegetable oil
2 tablespoons chiffonade fresh mint
1/4 cup tequila
1/4 cup sugar
Salt and black pepper to taste

In a very hot cast iron skillet, blacken citrus sections and shallot, turning constantly 1 minute. Place citrus in a medium bowl. Add vinegar, oil and mint to citrus mixture; reserve.

In a small skillet heat tequila and sugar. Use extreme caution to flambé mixture; ignite tequila by either tilting skillet towards flame on range or lighting with a long taper match.

Combine tequila syrup with reserved mixture; season with salt and pepper. Store in covered container in refrigerator up to 1 week.

Chef's Tip: If you have the chance, make this dressing with sweet Texas grapefruit such as Rio Star or Ruby Red.

## CRABMEAT RAVIGOTE AND FRIED GREEN TOMATOES

Yield: 4 servings

*Chef's Note: Ravigote is a classic sauce meaning "to perk it up." At Brennan's of Houston it means "to create raving compliments." Consider it the "Be All, End All" of salads!*

1 cup Ravigote Sauce (page 49)
1/2 cup Herb Vinaigrette
   (recipe follows)
1 pound jumbo lump crabmeat,
   cleaned and picked over
1 teaspoon Creole Seafood
   Seasoning
Vegetable oil for deep frying
   (optional)
2 parsnips, sliced paper thin with a
   peeler (optional)
1 beet, sliced paper thin with a
   peeler (optional)
Salt and black pepper to taste
12 Fried Green Tomato slices
   (recipe follows)
4 cups baby greens

Prepare Ravigote Sauce and Herb Vinaigrette; reserve until needed. In a small bowl, season crabmeat with Creole Seafood Seasoning and toss with Ravigote Sauce.

Heat oil in deep fryer to 350 degrees. Deep fry parsnips and beet until crisp, drain on paper towel and season chips with salt and pepper. Reserve until needed.

Prepare Fried Green Tomatoes; place 3 tomato slices positioned near the edge of each plate, leaving space in the plate's center. Top each slice with crabmeat. Toss greens with vinaigrette and place a mound in center of each plate. Top salad with reserved chips.

*Chef's Tip: Vegetable chips from the grocery also make excellent garnishes for this dish.*

## FRIED GREEN TOMATOES

Yield: 4 servings

*Chef's Note: This traditional Southern side dish is popular for using unripened tomatoes before Jack Frost visits.*

3 (medium size) green tomatoes,
   sliced 1/4-inch thick
Salt and black pepper to taste
1 egg
1/3 cup milk
1 cup all-purpose flour
1/2 cup yellow cornmeal
1/4 cup grated Parmesan cheese
3 tablespoons chopped fresh herbs
   (oregano, thyme and/or parsley)
1/2 cup vegetable oil

Season tomato slices with salt and pepper. Blend egg and milk in a small bowl.

Combine flour, cornmeal, cheese and herbs in a medium bowl. Dust tomato slices in flour mixture, then egg wash and back into flour mixture.

Heat oil in a medium skillet over medium-high heat; sauté tomatoes 1 to 2 minutes on each side, or until golden brown.

Drain slices on paper towels and place in ovenproof pan or microwavable dish. Reheat just before serving.

*Chef's Tip: If green tomatoes aren't available, ask your grocer for unripened tomatoes or use the firmest red tomatoes.*

## HERB VINAIGRETTE

Yield: 1 1/3 cups

1/4 cup finely chopped bell pepper
   (any color)
1/2 teaspoon minced garlic
2 teaspoons dry yellow mustard
2 teaspoons minced fresh oregano
1 teaspoon salt
1/2 teaspoon black pepper
3/4 cup vegetable oil
1/4 cup red wine vinegar

Mix bell pepper, garlic, mustard, oregano, salt, pepper, oil and vinegar together. Let vinaigrette macerate (infuse flavors) at least 24 hours before using.

Store in airtight container in refrigerator up to 3 weeks. Shake well before using.

*Chef's Tips: To add color, use a combination of green, red, yellow and/or orange bell peppers.*

**For flavor variety, substitute Dijon for dry yellow mustard.**

**Always use a good quality oil and vinegar when making vinaigrette.**

Crabmeat Ravigote and Fried Green Tomatoes

## RAVIGOTE SAUCE

Yield: 2½ cups

*Chef's Note: This classic is a cool, highly seasoned sauce that truly lifts the palate.*

1½ cups mayonnaise
⅔ cup Creole mustard
1 hard-cooked egg, chopped
2 tablespoons chopped capers
1 tablespoon chopped fresh herbs
   (basil, thyme or oregano)

1 tablespoon Louisiana hot
   pepper sauce
1 tablespoon Worcestershire sauce
Salt and black pepper to taste

Combine mayonnaise, mustard, egg, capers, herbs, hot sauce, and Worcestershire in medium bowl; blend well. Season with salt and pepper. Store in covered container in refrigerator up to 5 days.

Chef's Tip: This sauce is an integral component of Crabmeat Ravigote and Fried Green Tomatoes but also goes with Chicken-Fried Catfish (page 117) or with cold shrimp. In New Orleans, my colleague Chef Jamie Shannon, of Commander's Palace Restaurant, serves it hot to accompany succulent crab cakes — see his *Commander's Kitchen* cookbook.

## FAMILY, FRIENDS AND GUESTS SAY "CHEESE."

When arranging a cheese course or plate, there are so many cheese varieties that you can offer many options for texture and taste. That variety also means you can have cheese as an hors d'oeuvre, salad accompaniment or a dessert.

Try offering a trio of cheese types — from different types of milk like goat, sheep and cow.

At Brennan's of Houston, our cheese plates will also feature a soft-ripened cheese, such as a Camembert (ex. Old Chatham), a hard or semi-aged cheese, such as a white cheddar (ex. Cypress Grove), plus a blue-veined cheese (ex. Great Hill Blue).

By visiting your local market, grocery or gourmet shop, you can get acquainted with the many styles and flavors currently available — and get a free taste or two while you're at it.

Of course, we add extras to our cheese offerings. We adorn our cheese plates with fresh berries, dried fruit soaked in port, favorite nuts, honey, chocolate and a potpourri of breads and crackers.

## CRABMEAT SALAD FAULK

Yield: 6 servings

*Chef's Note: In another life this was a Salad Maison. We perfected the dish for a most special guest of Brennan's of Houston, Carolyn Faulk, and it is now a classic in its new re-christened form!*

3/4 cup Herb Vinaigrette, divided (page 48)
1 large red bell pepper
2 tablespoons vegetable oil
1 cup button, or assorted wild, mushrooms
1 teaspoon Creole Seafood Seasoning (page 157)
6 strips cooked bacon, crumbled
1/2 cup hearts of palm
1 medium avocado
Juice of 1 lemon
1 pound jumbo lump crabmeat, cleaned and picked over
2 dashes Louisiana hot pepper sauce
6 cups mixed baby greens
Salt and black pepper to taste
6 chives, cut into 1-inch lengths

Prepare Herb Vinaigrette; reserve until needed.

Roast bell pepper under broiler until heavily blistered. Place in a bowl, cover with plastic wrap and cool at least 10 minutes. With small knife, scrape skin off of pepper. Rub pepper with paper towel to remove seeds. Cut pepper into small dice to yield 3/4 cup; refrigerate until needed.

Heat oil in a large skillet; add mushrooms and seafood seasoning. Sauté until mushrooms start to brown and are heated through. Cool mushrooms; cut into quarters and refrigerate until needed.

Slice hearts of palm into half moons, 1/4-inch thick; refrigerate until needed. Peel avocado, cut into small dice to yield 1/2 cup and toss with lemon juice to help retain color.

In a large bowl, toss bell pepper, mushrooms, bacon, hearts of palm, avocado, crabmeat, hot sauce and 3 tablespoons reserved Herb Vinaigrette. Season with salt and pepper.

In another large bowl, toss greens with 3 tablespoons vinaigrette. Adjust seasonings. Divide greens among 6 plates and top each with 2/3 cup crabmeat mixture. Drizzle remaining 6 tablespoons vinaigrette over tops of salads; garnish with chives.

Chef's Tips: For a more dramatic presentation, press crabmeat mixture into a small cup or a 2-inch ring mold and invert onto greens.

Use canned or bottled pimientos for the roasted red bell pepper and a good quality, store-bought vinaigrette to save time in preparing this dish.

*"To eat is a necessity, to eat intelligently is an art"*
*— La Rochefoucauld*

Crabmeat Salad Faulk

Corn-Crusted Red Snapper Salad

52

## CORN-CRUSTED
## RED SNAPPER SALAD

Yield: 6 servings

*Chef's Note: This is a one-of-a-kind entrée salad with a distinctive corn crust and a roasted tomato and herb vinaigrette that is habit-forming.*

2 cups fresh corn kernels (about 4 medium ears of corn), divided
2 tablespoons finely diced red bell pepper

2 tablespoons finely diced red onion
1 tablespoon chopped fresh parsley
1 tablespoon cornstarch

Pulse 1 cup corn in food processor until about half puréed. Place partially puréed corn, remaining corn kernels, pepper, onion, parsley and cornstarch in a medium bowl. Combine thoroughly and set aside to use for crust.

1 cup Roasted Tomato Tarragon Vinaigrette, divided (page 53)
1 tablespoon Creole Seafood Seasoning (page 157)
6 (4-to 5-ounce) snapper fillets
1 cup all-purpose flour
2 teaspoons Creole Seafood Seasoning
3 egg whites, slightly whisked
1/2 cup vegetable oil
1/2 medium red onion, julienned
6 cups baby lettuces or a mixture of spring greens

Prepare Roasted Tomato Tarragon Vinaigrette; reserve. Preheat oven to 350 degrees.

Sprinkle 1 tablespoon seafood seasoning onto both sides of fillets. Combine flour and 2 teaspoons Creole Seafood Seasoning in a medium bowl or on a plate. Dredge fillets in seasoned flour and then egg whites, letting excess egg white drip off fish. Dredge again in seasoned flour; shake off excess. Using a fork, press corn mixture firmly on interior side of fillets.

Heat oil in a medium skillet over medium heat. Cook fish in batches of two. Carefully place two fillets with corn-crusted side down in oil by placing end of fish closest to you in skillet and letting the remainder fall away from you into the skillet. Cook until corn turns golden brown. (Be extremely careful with loose kernels in hot oil — they will pop like popcorn and oil may splatter.) Turn fillets over and cook on plain side 1 minute. Remove fillets from skillet and place on paper towels. After browning each batch, remove corn crust "debris" from skillet. Repeat cooking procedure with remaining fillets.

Place onion on a baking sheet; arrange fillets on top of onion. Finish fillets by baking 10 minutes, or until done in center. Remove fillets from oven, but keep warm until ready to use. Reserve caramelized onion from beneath fish for garnish.

Reserve 6 to 9 tablespoons Roasted Tomato Tarragon Vinaigrette to top fish. When ready to serve, toss together remaining vinaigrette with salad greens. Divide dressed greens among 6 plates, and nestle a fillet partially on top of each salad. Spoon caramelized onion over fish. Drizzle 1 to 1½ tablespoons reserved Roasted Tomato Tarragon Vinaigrette over fish and around the plate. For other extra accents, check the Chef's Tips below.

**Chef's Tips:** I've done a salad similar to this with eggplant diced about the size of a corn kernel.

Also, feel free to garnish this salad with other relishes that you can create, like pickled artichoke and cherry tomato. You probably have a great combination right in your fridge waiting to be tossed together.

## ROASTED TOMATO TARRAGON VINAIGRETTE

Yield: 1¼ cups

6 Roma tomatoes
2 teaspoons olive oil
Salt and black pepper to taste
1 teaspoon minced garlic
1 tablespoon minced shallots
2 tablespoons finely chopped fresh tarragon
3 tablespoons Creole mustard
2 tablespoons red wine vinegar
3/4 cup vegetable oil
Dash Tabasco
Splash of Pernod (a French anise or licorice liqueur) (optional)

Preheat broiler. Cut tomatoes in half lengthwise, drizzle with olive oil and season with salt and pepper. Place tomatoes on a jellyroll pan lightly sprayed with cooking spray and broil under low heat approximately 30 to 40 minutes, or until tomatoes lose more than half their juices. When checking tomatoes for doneness, use caution to avoid hot liquid splashing out. If tomatoes start to blacken, place pan on a lower shelf in the oven. Remove from oven and let cool. Coarsely chop tomatoes; set aside.

In a medium bowl, whisk together garlic, shallots, tarragon, mustard and vinegar. Slowly incorporate vegetable oil with a whisk into vinegar mixture. If mixture is too thick, add cold water 1 teaspoon at a time until desired consistency is reached. Mix in reserved tomatoes, Tabasco, salt, pepper and Pernod (if desired). Store in covered container in refrigerator up to 1 week.

**Chef's Tip:** If you feel like adding other fresh herbs, such as basil, be our guest!

Smith Street Cobb Salad

## SMITH STREET COBB SALAD

Yield: 4 servings

*Chef's Note: Guests swoon at our tableside presentation of this timeless classic from Hollywood's Brown Derby Restaurant.*

1 1/2 cups Creamy Dill Dressing (recipe follows)
1 pound (26/30 count) shrimp, peeled and deveined
1 tablespoon vegetable oil
Creole Seafood Seasoning (page 157) to taste
8 cups chiffonade Romaine lettuce
4 hard-cooked eggs, finely chopped
8 slices bacon, cooked crisp and chopped
4 Roma tomatoes, diced
1 cup crumbled blue cheese
1 avocado, coarsely chopped

Prepare Creamy Dill Dressing; refrigerate until needed. Rub shrimp with oil and seasoning. Or, sauté in a medium skillet over medium-high heat 2 to 3 minutes, until shrimp are pink and done. Cool and chop.

Place lettuce in bottom of a large salad bowl. Arrange shrimp, eggs, bacon, tomatoes, cheese, and avocado in neat rows across top of greens; cover with plastic wrap until ready to serve. To serve, present arranged salad to guests; drizzle reserved Creamy Dill Dressing over salad. Toss and serve on chilled plates.

Chef's Tip:  If seafood doesn't work for you, don't deny yourself this great salad. Substitute grilled chicken or turkey cut into 1/2-inch cubes.

## CREAMY DILL DRESSING

Yield 1 1/2 cups

1 cup mayonnaise
1/4 cup sour cream
1/4 cup white vinegar
1 tablespoon minced shallots
1 teaspoon minced garlic
1 tablespoon minced fresh dill
Salt to taste
Fine grind black pepper to taste

Combine mayonnaise, sour cream, vinegar, shallots, garlic and dill in a small bowl. Season with salt and pepper.

Store in covered container in refrigerator up to 5 days.

Chef's Tip: Substitute 1 to 2 tablespoons prepared horseradish for the dill and enjoy a great horseradish dip.

## BEEFSTEAK TOMATO AND CRABMEAT SALAD

Yield: 4 servings

*Chef's Note: Nothing says summer more than a perfect beefsteak tomato piled high with supreme crabmeat and dressed with a fresh herb vinaigrette.*

3/4 cup Herb Vinaigrette, divided
    (page 48)
1/2 gallon water
4 large beefsteak tomatoes
Salt and black pepper to taste
1 pound jumbo lump crabmeat,
    cleaned and picked over
8 cups mixed baby greens
Pickled beets, carrots, baby corn
    or favorite marinated vegetables
    for garnish

Prepare Herb Vinaigrette; reserve until needed. Bring water to a boil in a large stockpot over high heat.

Use a paring knife to score tomatoes on the bottom with a small X and remove stem section from tomato. Drop tomatoes into boiling water about 1 minute, just until skin begins to peel away. Immediately immerse tomatoes into a bowl of ice water; when cool, remove skins.

Place tomatoes on a cutting board, and use a paring knife to cut into middle of tomato in a zig-zag fashion all the way around making a crown pattern. Separate tomato halves and gently scoop out insides; season interior with salt and pepper.

In a medium bowl, gently toss crabmeat with 1/4 cup Herb Vinaigrette. Fill tomato halves with crabmeat. In another medium bowl toss greens with remaining 1/2 cup Herb Vinaigrette.

To serve, place a mound of dressed greens in center of each plate; top with 2 tomato halves. Garnish with pickled beets, carrots, corn or your favorite marinated vegetables.

Chef's Tip: If you don't have crabmeat, serve with shrimp tossed in Ravigote Sauce (page 49) or Remoulade Sauce (page 31).

Beefsteak Tomato and Crabmeat Salad

# FRIED CRAWFISH SALAD

Yield: 6 servings

*Chef's Note: As we anticipate crawfish season, this is one dish we long to dive into. The hot-fried crawfish tails over the honey mustard-dressed greens rocket you into culinary orbit.*

3/4 cup Honey Mustard Dressing, divided (page 57)
Vegetable oil for deep frying
3 cups crawfish tail meat
3 tablespoons Creole Seafood Seasoning, (page 157) divided
3 cups all-purpose flour
3 eggs
1 cup milk
12 cups mixed baby greens
12 pickled okra pods, sliced to form fans
Optional garnishes: Dad's Hush Puppies (page 147) or vegetable relishes

Prepare Honey Mustard Dressing; reserve until needed.

Preheat oil in deep fryer to 350 degrees.

Season crawfish with 2½ tablespoons Creole Seafood Seasoning and dust with flour. In a small bowl, combine eggs and milk. Dip crawfish into egg wash and dredge back into flour.

Deep-fry crawfish until they float to the top, about 2 minutes.

Remove and drain on paper towels. Sprinkle with remaining ½ tablespoon Creole Seafood Seasoning to taste.

Toss greens and ½ cup reserved Honey Mustard Dressing together in a large bowl.

Chef Carl Walker and former Sous Chef, Mark Holley

To serve, place a mound of dressed greens in center of each large plate, top with ½ cup fried crawfish tails and garnish with 2 okra pods. You may wish to add some vegetable relishes. Drizzle crawfish with remaining ¼ cup dressing. Serve with Dad's Hush Puppies (page 147).

Chef's Tip: Another great salad combination is to top this salad with fried oysters dredged in the same seasoned flour, and the greens with the Creamy Dill Dressing (page 54).

## Honey Mustard Dressing

Yield: 1 cup

*Chef's Note: This is a zippy version using Creole mustard!*

1 teaspoon minced shallots
1 teaspoon minced garlic
1 egg or pasteurized equivalent
1/4 cup Creole mustard
2 1/2 tablespoons cider vinegar
2 tablespoons honey
1 teaspoon salt
Pinch white pepper
1/2 cup vegetable oil
2 teaspoons chopped
   fresh tarragon
Dash Tabasco

Place shallots, garlic, egg, mustard, vinegar, honey, salt and pepper in food processor; blend. With motor running, slowly add oil until mixture is emulsified.

Blend in tarragon and Tabasco. Store in covered container in refrigerator up to 3 days.

## Smoked Chicken Salad

Yield: 4 servings

*Chef's Note: What a blue ribbon way to use a smoked chicken. It's one of Alex Brennan-Martin's favorite entrée salads. In Texas, we smoke lots of "Dancing Chickens"! Slide a seasoned chicken over an open 16-ounce can of beer (tall-boy) and stand it in the smoker. When you open the smoker doors at the end of the cooking time, with some imagination — or after you drink the rest of the tall-boys — you'll think that those chickens are dancin'. I've learned my smoking tricks from my friend Ray Burgess.*

1 Smoked Chicken (recipe follows)
4 eggs, deviled (8 halves)
1 cup Mama's Bacon Dressing, divided (page 44)
1 roasted red bell pepper, julienned
1 roasted green bell pepper, julienned
1 roasted yellow bell pepper, julienned
1 pound spinach leaves, washed, dried and destemmed
8 button mushrooms, quartered

Smoke chicken; debone and refrigerate in covered container up to 2 days before use.

Prepare deviled eggs; reserve in covered container in refrigerator up to 1 day before use.

Prepare Mama's Bacon Dressing; reserve until needed.

Roast bell peppers. See Chef's Tip, page 112 for instructions.

In a large bowl toss spinach, peppers and mushrooms in 2/3 cup Mama's Bacon Dressing. Divide spinach mixture evenly among 4 salad plates. Toss shredded chicken with remaining 1/3 cup dressing in same bowl; pile chicken on top of spinach. Garnish each plate with 2 deviled eggs.

## Smoked Chicken

Yield: 1 whole chicken

1 (3-pound) fryer chicken
2 tablespoons Creole Meat Seasoning (page 156)
2 tablespoons molasses

Rinse chicken under running water. Remove and discard giblets. Season chicken with Creole Meat Seasoning and rub outside with molasses.

Place in a smoker using your favorite wood and smoke until chicken reaches an internal temperature of 165 degrees when tested with a meat thermometer. Cool chicken; discard skin and bones.

Shred chicken into bite-size pieces. Refrigerate in covered container until ready to use.

*"Part of the secret of success in life is to eat what you like and let the food fight it out inside."*

*— Mark Twain*

## Asparagus Crab Vichyssoise

Yield: 6 servings

*Chef's Note: Take the steam out of hot weather by serving this easy-to-make, refreshing first course topped with jumbo lump blue crab.*

2 bunches large asparagus
   (about 2 pounds)
2 tablespoons vegetable oil
3/4 cup coarsely chopped onion
1 1/2 cups coarsely chopped leeks
1 tablespoon minced garlic
6 cups crab stock, fish stock,
   or water
1 1/2 cups coarsely chopped
   potatoes
1/4 teaspoon liquid crab boil
   seasoning
1 cup packed spinach, cleaned,
   stemmed and patted or spun dry
2 teaspoons salt
1 teaspoon black pepper
1 pound jumbo lump crabmeat,
   cleaned and picked over
Plain yogurt as desired

Cut 30 asparagus tips, about 1 1/2 inches long, from stalks to use for garnish; reserve. Dice remainder of stalks into 1/2-inch pieces to be used for soup; reserve. In a large saucepan of boiling water, quickly cook asparagus tips until just tender-crisp. Immediately drain tips and immerse in a large bowl filled with ice water. When tips are completely chilled, remove from water and drain on paper towels; reserve in refrigerator.

Heat oil in a large saucepan over medium heat; add onion and leeks. Sweat onion until it starts to turn transparent. Add garlic and cook 1 minute.

Add stock, reserved diced asparagus, potatoes and crab boil seasoning. Bring to a boil and simmer 15 minutes, or until potatoes are tender. Cool.

In batches, place vegetables in blender and add spinach a little at a time. Purée, then strain into a large storage container. Season with salt and pepper; cover and refrigerate until soup is completely chilled, about 3 to 4 hours. Once chilled, check soup again for seasoning, adjusting if necessary. Ladle into chilled soup bowls.

Garnish each serving with reserved asparagus tips and a heaping tablespoon of crabmeat and yogurt in the center.

Chef's Tips: Always read a recipe completely before making it. For example, if some of the ingredients will be put into a blender or food processor, you can generally cut or chop the food into larger size pieces.

When removing blanched vegetables from boiling water, put them into a bowl of ice water to stop any further cooking — this is often referred to as "shocking." However, don't shock root vegetables because they tend to absorb water — just drain.

Instead of making homemade fish stock, substitute frozen fish stock, which is available at some grocery stores.

## Gumbo YaYa

Yield: 1 gallon, 16 (1-cup) servings

*Chef's Note: My first introduction to Creole food, and a brown roux, was at Mr. B's almost 20 years ago. It's Mr. B's signature soup and has become one of my personal favorites.*

1 recipe Chicken 'N Stock (page 69)
1 1/2 cups Brown Roux (page 68)
2 pounds andouille or spicy
   smoked sausage
1 tablespoon vegetable oil
1 tablespoon minced garlic
1 large green bell pepper, chopped
1 large red bell pepper, chopped
1 medium yellow onion, chopped
2 tablespoons Louisiana hot
   pepper sauce
2 tablespoons Worcestershire sauce
2 tablespoons salt
1 teaspoon black pepper
2 cups cooked white rice

Prepare Chicken 'N Stock. Prepare Brown Roux; reserve until needed.

Slice sausage 1/4-inch thick; cut into half moons. Heat oil in a large stockpot over medium-high heat; add sausage and render until it starts to brown and fat is cooked out. Add garlic, green and red bell peppers and onion; saute 3 minutes, or until vegetables are tender. Pour in reserved stock and bring to a simmer.

Add reserved roux, whisking vigorously until roux is incorporated. Reduce heat to low and simmer 30 to 45 minutes.

Stir in chicken, hot sauce, Worcestershire, salt and pepper.

Serve in individual bowls; top with hot rice.

Gumbo YaYa

## TURTLE SOUP

Yield: 2½ quarts

*Chef's Note: Turtle soup is unquestionably the most popular dish at Brennan's of Houston. We make 35-gallon batches in pots the size of small bathtubs. And we only use freshwater turtles, such as snapping turtles — not the environmentally threatened sea turtles! We never attend any outside functions, such as charity events, without bringing kettles of turtle soup for guests to taste. Most diners claim this is the best soup EVER!*

2 tablespoons vegetable oil
1½ pounds turtle meat, chili or
    large grind
1½ tablespoons Creole Seafood
    Seasoning (page 157)
1½ tablespoons Creole Meat
    Seasoning (page 156)
1 cup finely chopped onion
1 cup finely chopped green
    bell pepper
½ cup finely chopped celery
1 tablespoon minced garlic
½ teaspoon crushed dry thyme
2 bay leaves
8 cups Veal Stock (page 69) (or substitute canned no-salt beef broth)
¾ cup tomato purée
½ cup vegetable oil
½ cup all-purpose flour
1 cup dry sherry
2 tablespoons Louisiana hot
    pepper sauce
2 tablespoons Worcestershire sauce
Juice of 1 lemon
5 ounces fresh spinach, stems
    removed, washed, patted dry,
    coarsely chopped
2 hard-cooked eggs, finely chopped
Dry sherry for garnish (optional)

Heat 2 tablespoons oil in a large stockpot over medium-high heat. Brown meat along with Creole Seafood and Creole Meat Seasonings; cook about 20 minutes, or until liquid is almost evaporated.

Add onion, bell pepper, celery and garlic while stirring constantly. Add thyme and bay leaves; reduce heat to medium and sauté (stirring frequently) 20 to 25 minutes, or until vegetables are tender and start to caramelize.

Add stock and tomato purée; bring to a boil. Reduce heat and simmer uncovered 30 minutes, periodically skimming away any fat that rises to the top.

While stock is simmering, make roux. Heat ½ cup oil over medium heat in a small saucepan. Add flour, a little at a time, stirring constantly with a wooden spoon — being careful not to burn the roux.

After flour is added, cook about 3 minutes, until roux smells nutty, is pale in color, and the consistency of wet sand.

Using a whisk, vigorously stir roux into soup, a little at a time to prevent lumping. Simmer uncovered about 25 minutes, stirring occasionally to prevent sticking on the bottom.

Add sherry and bring to a boil. Add hot sauce and Worcestershire; reduce heat and simmer 30 minutes or until starchy flavor is gone, skimming any fat or foam that rises to the top.

Add lemon juice; return to a simmer 15 to 20 minutes.

Add spinach and chopped egg; bring to a simmer and adjust seasoning with seafood seasoning or salt. Remove bay leaves before ladling into bowls.

When we serve the soup, we add a splash of sherry on top.

Chef's Tips: Check the Source Guide for turtle meat.

For mock turtle soup: substitute ground beef or a combination of half ground beef/ half ground veal in chili grind.

*"In France, cooking is a serious art form and a national sport."*

*— Julia Child*

## TASSO HAM AND ANDOUILLE SAUSAGE

Besides having big gardens, my parents and my grandparents processed their own meat. When the weather cooled, neighbors gathered to butcher hogs. My dad and my grandpa would salt-cure the hams and bacon and then hang them in the smokehouse — no heat, but enough smoke to penetrate the meat. Then the hams would get wrapped and hang until some event called for them to be cut down and polished.

You'll notice in many of our dishes we use tasso ham or andouille sausage. We think these native Cajun ingredients make our dishes special. However, we recognize that you may not have access to them at all times. Check the Source Guide (page 186) for supplies.

For tasso ham alternatives, look in your grocer's deli for a Cajun spiced ham. Nearly any spicy, smoked sausage like chorizo or hot Italian sausage will work well if you choose not to use andouille.

## BUTTERNUT SQUASH SOUP

Yield: 6 servings

*Chef's Note: When we think of fall, we yearn for this ideal autumn soup. Its seasonal color, roasted squash flavor, and andouille spiciness will have you praying it's September soon!*

2 (1 1/2 pounds) butternut squash
Vegetable oil, divided
3 cups chicken stock, or canned chicken broth, divided
1 teaspoon minced garlic
1/4 cup chopped onion
1/2 cup finely chopped andouille sausage or spicy smoked sausage
1 teaspoon Louisiana hot pepper sauce
1 teaspoon Worcestershire sauce
Dash ground nutmeg
Creole Meat Seasoning (page 156) to taste
Brown sugar to taste
Salt and black pepper to taste
12 (1/4 inch) slices andouille or spicy smoked sausage,
1 Granny Smith apple, peeled and chopped
Plain yogurt for garnish

Preheat oven to 350 degrees.

Cut squash in half lengthwise and remove seeds. Rub just enough oil to coat squash and place flesh side down onto a baking pan. Roast squash in oven 45 to 60 minutes, or until tender. Remove pulp. Use 4 cups to purée in blender with 1 cup chicken stock.

In a medium saucepan, sauté garlic, onion and chopped sausage in 1 tablespoon oil until tender. Add squash pulp, hot sauce, Worcestershire, nutmeg, Creole Meat Seasoning and remaining 2 cups chicken stock.

Bring to a boil, reduce heat and simmer 10 to 15 minutes. At this point, check soup for flavor and consistency. Add brown sugar, salt and pepper to taste. If soup seems a little thin, cook until reduced to desired consistency or add extra squash pulp.

Render sausage slices in a little oil in a small skillet over medium heat until beginning to brown. Add apple and sauté just until tender.

Ladle soup into bowls and garnish top with apple/sausage mixture and yogurt.

---

### GARNISHING A PLATE

To make zig-zag lines when garnishing a plate, put yogurt or sauce in a squeeze bottle. Or, for a disposable container, put garnish into a zip-lock bag. Snip off corner of bag and squeeze away!

---

## CREOLE ONION SOUP

Yield: 8 cups

*Chef's Note: Often, Creole Onion Soup is the Soup du Jour — it is especially popular at our brunches.*

1/4 cup vegetable oil
4 cups julienned yellow onions
1/4 cup all-purpose flour
5 cups beef broth
2 tablespoons brandy
2 tablespoons Louisiana hot pepper sauce
2 tablespoons Worcestershire sauce
1 cup shredded pepper Jack cheese (optional)
Salt and black pepper to taste

Butternut Squash Soup

Heat oil in a large stockpot over high heat.

Once it starts to smoke, add onions, reduce heat to medium-high and sauté until caramelized or browned.

Remove from heat and add flour; stir until flour is absorbed and there aren't any lumps.

Add broth, brandy, hot sauce and Worcestershire. Return to heat and cook until soup reaches a medium simmer. Continue to simmer 15 to 20 minutes. If desired, stir cheese into soup until melted.

Season with salt and pepper.

Ladle hot soup into bowls.

Chef's Tip: This soup is best when made with Texas 1015 onions, named for the October date advised for planting. We like to melt either Monterey Jack or sharp Cheddar cheese on top. To further embellish this soup, sprinkle some spicy croutons over the top.

## Lobster Dome Bisque

Yield: 8 (1-cup) servings

*Chef's Note: The drama of the puff pastry dome bisque is a must during our December holiday season.*

2 (1¼-pound) live lobsters
1 gallon boiling water
3 tablespoons salt
1 cup melted unsalted butter
1 cup all-purpose flour
2 tablespoons vegetable oil
2 cups coarsely chopped onion
1 cup coarsely chopped carrot
¾ cup coarsely chopped celery
5 tablespoons tomato paste
½ tablespoon black peppercorns
2 garlic cloves, finely chopped
1 bay leaf
1 sprig of fresh thyme
½ cup brandy
½ cup dry white wine
1½ cups whipping cream
1 tablespoon dry vermouth
1 tablespoon brandy
Salt and black pepper to taste
2 to 3 packages puff pastry sheets, thawed, flattened and re-frozen
1 egg yolk mixed with 1 tablespoon cold water, reserved in refrigerator for later use
Paprika and minced fresh parsley or finely snipped chives for optional garnish

In a large stockpot bring water and salt to a boil. Ease live lobsters into boiling water and simmer about 10 minutes. Remove lobsters from water to cool. Reserve cooking water. When lobster is cool, break apart by first twisting tail from head. Use a knife or kitchen shears to remove tail meat. Remove claws from body. Use kitchen shears and a mallet to crack the claws; extract meat from the claws and knuckles that run from the claw to the body. Cut lobster meat into bite-size pieces and reserve in a covered container in refrigerator. Break down lobster shell and body into smaller pieces; reserve.

In a small saucepan melt butter. Stir in flour to make a roux. Cook over low to medium heat about 10 minutes. Remove from heat; reserve.

Heat oil in another large (6-quart) stockpot; sweat onion, carrot and celery until onion becomes translucent.

Add lobster shell to vegetables. Mix in tomato paste, peppercorns, garlic, bay leaf and thyme sprig; sauté 5 minutes. Pour in ½ cup brandy and wine. Cook 5 minutes over medium heat. Add reserved poaching water to pot and bring to a simmer. Slowly whisk in reserved roux until roux is dissolved into the broth, leaving no lumps. Simmer about 20 minutes on low heat to cook out flour taste of the roux.

Strain soup base through a fine mesh strainer, pushing down on the lobster and vegetable mixture to extract all the flavor and liquid. If you think the soup is too thick, thin down with a little water. The soup should be a medium creamy consistency.

Pour in cream and return soup to a low simmer. Add vermouth and 1 tablespoon brandy. You may add extra alcohol at this point to bring out flavor of the lobster. Taste the bisque before adding any salt since the poaching liquid may be salty. Adjust salt and pepper seasoning.

To serve immediately without a dome, ladle soup into cups. Heat reserved lobster meat and garnish tops of soup with lobster and parsley or chives and a sprinkle of paprika.

To serve with a dome, remove soup from heat. Chill until cold, at least 2 hours.

For baking you will need 6 to 8 oven-proof ramekins or cups, each holding 6 to 8 ounces. Place ramekin or cup on puff pastry as a measuring guide. Use a knife to cut circles in the frozen puff pastry, leaving a ½- to ¾-inch margin of pastry around edge of ramekin. Cut out enough circles of pastry to equal servings you need; set aside.

Divide reserved lobster evenly among serving cups, placing in bottom of each cup. Ladle cold soup into cups, filling to within ¼-inch from the rim. One side of pastry will be more moist than the other once thawing starts. Place the more moist side down over top of soup so it will help stick to the cup. Fold edges down over rim of cup, pressing dough firmly, with your fingers or palms of your hands, to sides of cup. Cover lightly with plastic wrap and refrigerate soup cups until ready to bake. May be prepared up to 2 to 4 hours ahead of baking.

Preheat oven to 375 degrees. Using a pastry brush, brush top of pastry domes with egg wash. Place cups on a tray and put in oven 25 to 30 minutes to heat. Soup is ready when the pastry rises into a dome and starts to brown, or when some of the soup leaks out around the side. Insert an instant-read thermometer through pastry into center of the soup to check temperature. When soup reaches 185 degrees, remove from oven.

Sprinkle domes with paprika and parsley. We present our bisque cups on a plate lined with a doily or decoratively folded napkin. Serve immediately.

**Chef's Tips: Always buy lively lobsters! For added seafood flavor, some stores carry lobster or shrimp base or bouillon cubes.**

**Add base or bouillon to the soup before seasoning with salt since most flavored bases tend to be salty. A splash of vermouth or brandy also enhances the flavor.**

65

Lobster Dome Bisque

*"Only the pure of heart can make a good soup."*
*— Ludwig von Beethoven*

## SEAFOOD GUMBO

Yield: 8 (1½-cups) servings

*Chef's Note: Although a gumbo, this recipe is roux-less. In the late '70s and early '80s, Ella Brennan set out to re-define Creole cuisine. Her goal was to transform all the heavy sauces and soups to haute Creole, which would lighten the look of the food, while still packing it full of flavor!*

*Choctaw Indians from Louisiana are said to have been the first to use filé powder, a spice made of ground dried sassafras tree leaves, which contributes a thickening agent as well as flavor. When I was young, we used the roots for sassafras tea at breakfast time.*

2 medium onions, coarsely chopped
2 green bell peppers, coarsely
  chopped
2 tablespoons minced garlic
1 tablespoon vegetable oil
2 teaspoons dried thyme
2 tablespoons shrimp base
  (optional)
1 (14.5-ounce) can diced tomatoes
6 tablespoons Louisiana
  hot pepper sauce
6 tablespoons Worcestershire sauce
4 tablespoons Creole Seafood
  Seasoning (page 157)
1 bay leaf
1 pound frozen cut okra
1½ teaspoons filé powder
1 quart seafood stock or water
1½ cups raw oysters, shucked
1 pound (36/42 count) shrimp,
  peeled and deveined
1 pound crabmeat or cubed fresh
  fish fillets
Hot cooked rice

In a large stockpot over medium-low heat, sauté onion, bell pepper and garlic in oil 15 to 20 minutes. Add thyme, shrimp base, tomatoes, hot sauce, Worcestershire, Creole Seafood Seasoning and bay leaf; cook 10 minutes.

Add okra and filé powder; cook 5 minutes. Add stock, oysters, shrimp and crabmeat; simmer 15 to 20 minutes, or until seafood is cooked through. Remove bay leaf before serving over hot cooked rice.

**Chef's Tip:** At the restaurant, we make the gumbo base, and add the filé powder to use as needed. We add the appropriate amount of stock and seafood to the refrigerated base, heat and serve. This can be done up to 2 days in advance.

## ROASTED PEANUT SOUP WITH HONEY-CAYENNE SHRIMP

Yield: 8 (1-cup) servings

*Chef's Note: We're eternally grateful to former Sous Chef James Koonce, a Louisiana boy and a gifted cook, for sharing this amazing soup with us.*

5 Roma tomatoes, halved
½ large onion
½ green bell pepper, coarsely
  chopped
½ rib celery, coarsely chopped
5 garlic cloves, crushed
½ cup peanuts
3½ tablespoons vegetable oil,
  divided
1¼ quarts chicken stock or water
3 tablespoons Louisiana hot
  pepper sauce
3 tablespoons Worcestershire sauce
¾ cup tomato juice
1 cup creamy peanut butter
Salt and black pepper to taste
Creole Seafood Seasoning (page 157)
16 (16/20 count) shrimp, peeled
  and deveined
Pinch cayenne pepper to taste
¼ cup honey

Preheat oven to 350 degrees. In a medium bowl, toss tomatoes, onion, bell pepper, celery, garlic and peanuts in 1½ tablespoons oil; spread on a baking sheet and roast 20 minutes, or until vegetables are tender. Place vegetables in a large stockpot; add stock, hot sauce, Worcestershire and tomato juice. Simmer 30 to 40 minutes. Whisk in peanut butter. In batches, purée mixture in a blender or food processor.

Strain soup into a clean stockpot, bring to a simmer, and season with salt, pepper and Creole Seafood Seasoning. Season shrimp with Creole Seafood Seasoning and a pinch of cayenne. Heat remaining 2 tablespoons oil in a medium skillet over medium-high heat; sauté shrimp until pink. Add honey and cook until syrupy. Ladle soup into individual bowls and garnish each serving with 2 honeyed shrimp. After arranging shrimp in bowl, drizzle remaining syrup from skillet over soup.

*"After a good dinner, one can forgive anyone, even one's own relations."*

*— Oscar Wilde*

Seafood Gumbo

## THAT ROUX IS BURNED!

Even though I grew up in Mark Twain country — he the Southern gentleman of the Mississippi River era — I didn't know much about the Louisiana nectar, roux. In the Marines, I'd worked with a gunnery sargent from South Carolina who always wanted the roux dark, but it wasn't until I went to work at Mr. B's as a sous chef in 1982 that I was really exposed to roux-making. Once I tried to convince the cooks that it was burnt. I eventually learned the nuances of roux-making from the best: Floyd Bealer, Jimmy Smith, and Malcom Soileau.

Be very careful when you are making a roux. We all wear long sleeves and cotton gloves to protect us from splashing hot oil and flour.

## BAYOU GUMBO

Yield: 2 quarts

*Chef's Note: Hats off to Creole chef Jose Arevalo for creating this triple "threat" gumbo of alligator, crawfish, and oysters, combined with a Brown Roux — Bayou City eating at its tastiest.*

1 cup Brown Roux (recipe follows)
1/2 pound alligator sausage
2 tablespoons vegetable oil
1 cup chopped onion
1 tablespoon minced garlic
2 cups (1/4-inch slices) okra
1 cup chopped green bell pepper
1 tablespoon Louisiana hot
   pepper sauce
1 tablespoon Worcestershire sauce
8 cups chicken stock (page 69) or
   canned chicken broth
1 1/2 teaspoons salt
1/2 teaspoon black pepper
1/2 pound fresh oysters, shucked
1 pound crawfish tail meat
2 teaspoons filé powder
3 cups hot cooked rice

Prepare Brown Roux; reserve.
  Slice sausage 1/4 inch thick and then cut into half moons.
  Heat oil in a stockpot over medium-high heat. Add sausage; sauté. Add onion and garlic; cook until onion becomes translucent.
  Add okra, bell pepper, hot sauce and Worcestershire; sauté until vegetables are tender.
  Stir in stock, salt and pepper; bring to boil. Add reserved Brown Roux, reduce heat to low and simmer 25 to 30 minutes. Add oysters and crawfish; simmer until oysters are curled around edges and cooked through, about 7 to 8 minutes. Stir in filé and ladle gumbo into individual bowls; top with rice.

Chef's Tip: Check the Source Guide for seafood that isn't available at your local market.

## BROWN ROUX

Yield: 4 cups

*Chef's Note: A Creole or Cajun-style brown roux isn't always used only for thickening purposes. Flavor is what you're trying to add to gumbos, and the roux may appear to be almost black, yet it is not burned. Other Louisiana dishes use a dark reddish-brown roux.*

2 cups vegetable oil
3 cups all-purpose flour, divided
1/3 cup finely chopped yellow onion
1/3 cup finely chopped green
   bell pepper
1/3 cup finely chopped celery
1 teaspoon minced garlic

In a heavy bottomed 4-quart stockpot, add oil and heat to smoking point. BE CAREFUL! Add flour in 1/4 cup increments to oil, letting flour become a dark nutty brown before adding next 1/4 cup flour.
  Continue to stir with a stiff whisk throughout whole process without letting flour burn on bottom of pot. When flour is all incorporated and deep brown, remove from heat and immediately add onion, pepper, celery and garlic. This will start to cool off the roux, bringing out more color and adding flavor.
  Put roux into another pan and cool. Cover and refrigerate until needed. Some of the oil will rise to the top; mix it back in when ready to use. May be stored in covered container in refrigerator up to 2 weeks.

Chef's Tips: When making a brown roux, always use a heavy saucepan — cast iron works well. Be sure it's dry and use the longest whisk or wooden spoon that you have. When making a large batch of roux, I sometimes wear cotton gloves to keep from burning myself while stirring the pot.

Try not to leave roux while it is cooking. If you have an emergency and must slip away, turn off the heat and give the pot a good stir to somewhat cool the mixture before leaving. If you end up getting black specks in your roux, let it cool before discarding and start over.

Every Creole chef seems to have a different idea as to the color of the roux when it is done, depending on its use.

## CHICKEN 'N STOCK

Yield: 3-4 cups boneless chicken/ 1 gallon stock

1 (3-pound) chicken
2 bay leaves
3 garlic cloves
1 rib celery, cut into large pieces
1 medium yellow onion, cut into large pieces
1 1/2 gallons water

Rinse chicken with cold water. Remove giblets and excess fat.

Place chicken, bay leaves, garlic, celery, onion, and water in a large stockpot. Bring to a simmer over medium-high heat; reduce heat and simmer about 45 minutes, or until chicken is cooked through. Remove chicken from stock and cool until it can be handled. Strain stock through a fine strainer and reserve.

Discard skin and debone chicken. Pull and shred chicken meat into bite size pieces; reserve until ready to use.

## BEEF OR VEAL STOCK

Yield: 1 gallon

8 pounds beef neck bones (veal bones for veal stock)
2 cups chopped onion
1 cup chopped celery
1 cup chopped carrot
1/2 cup tomato purée
1 head garlic, peeled and split
1 teaspoon dried thyme
2 bay leaves
1 tablespoon whole black peppercorns
6 quarts cold water, divided
1 cup red wine

Preheat oven to 400 degrees. Place bones in a large roasting pan, stirring and turning occasionally, about 1 hour, or until brown. When bones are browned, add onion, celery, carrot and tomato purée on top. Continue browning bones in oven, stirring occasionally, 20 minutes.

Place bones and vegetables in a large stockpot with garlic, thyme, bay leaves and peppercorns. Add 1 quart water to roasting pan and return pan to medium heat on range top. Deglaze pan by scraping bottom of pan until all the drippings are loosened. Add drippings to stockpot.

Add remaining 5 quarts water and wine to cover bones in stockpot. Bring water and bones to a boil; reduce heat to low and simmer 6 to 8 hours. Periodically check stock and skim off fat that rises to the top. When finished, strain stock. Discard bones and vegetables; reserve stock.

Place in refrigerator until completely cooled. Store in a covered airtight container in refrigerator up to 1 week, or freeze up to 2 months.

## DEMI-GLACÉ

In a medium saucepan over medium-high heat, bring stock to a rolling boil. Reduce heat to a simmer, skim periodically and let stock reduce until thick enough to coat the back of a spoon. Yield: 2 cups

Chef's Tips: Making homemade stock is well worth the effort for a truly outstanding flavored sauce or soup. Beef neck bones are easily found in the grocery store. You can also reduce the stock to a demi-glacé (directions above).

For a thrifty meal after making stock, there is usually enough meat on the neck bones to pick off and use in a quick hash or stew.

During hunting season, I process my own venison and substitute venison bones for the beef or veal. I cook it down until almost a demi-glacé consistency and then freeze for future use.

If you don't have the time to make demi-glacé, some gourmet stores sell it. The frozen, no-salt, no-MSG variety is best to me. The Source Guide lists an ideal place to purchase.

I t's only fitting in a New Orleans-style building situated in the Bayou City that Creole Jazz Brunch at Brennan's of Houston is a four-star tradition. Our foyer, lounges and courtyard are filled with fresh flowers. Tantalizing jazz music floats through the dining rooms as we proudly welcome guests with creative dishes and decorations.

We not only offer the classic breakfast/brunch tastes, but imaginative new versions of the old favorites like Eggs Benedict. We rely on our Southern mainstays — seafood and tasso ham and andouille sausage — to complement the many egg dishes. Undoubtedly, the sauces — like Hollandaise Sauce — that accompany these dishes are first-rate, top-notch — every superlative that can be attached to tasty Creole cuisine.

Our Sunday brunches welcome and satisfy our friends and their guests as they celebrate, visit and mark special occasions like Mother's Day and Easter — two immensely popular days to brunch with Brennan's of Houston. This past Easter, my teen-age sons, Engel and Brandon, assisted the big Easter bunny with his basket of real bunnies during the photograph sessions for young and not-so-young diners. Our guests and employees have watched my children grow up — just as we've watched our guests' children grow up, marry and have children of their own. It's certainly fitting that our restaurant, steeped in its own family traditions, should regularly welcome generations of the same family on countless Sundays throughout the year.

creole jazz brunch

71

Soft-Shell Crabs with
Eggs and Choron Sauce

## EGGS BENEDICT NEW CREOLE STYLE

Yield: 4 servings

*Chef's Notes: In 19 years of working with the Brennan family, I have seen this dish transformed several times. The original version was served on a Holland Rusk, which is now a rarity. From there we moved to English muffins and Canadian bacon, which enjoyed immense popularity. Last year, Alex's new idea added creativity and quality to this dish. Since we make our own tasso ham, we thinly slice the tasso, roll it up pinwheel style in puff pastry and bake the pinwheels like cinnamon rolls. One of my current weekend addictions is one of these pinwheels, topped with a little Creole Choron Sauce (page 153).*

1 sheet frozen puff pastry, thawed
3 tablespoons unsalted butter, melted
1/8 teaspoon cayenne pepper
1/2 teaspoon paprika
12 ounces tasso or Cajun spiced deli ham, thinly sliced
8 Poached Eggs (page 79)
2 cups Hollandaise Sauce (page 152)

Preheat oven to 350 degrees. Unfold puff pastry dough. Combine butter with cayenne and paprika. Brush one side of dough with 2 tablespoons seasoned butter. Place tasso lengthwise over three fourths of buttered dough. Roll pastry lengthwise to form a long jelly-roll. Cut roll into 8 pieces, each about 1 1/2-inches long. Use remaining 1 tablespoon seasoned butter to brush pastry edges of each roll.

Place rolls on a parchment-lined baking sheet or a baking sheet sprayed with nonstick spray. Bake 15 to 20 minutes, or until golden brown and cooked through.

Prepare Poached Eggs; keep warm. Prepare Hollandaise Sauce; keep warm. To serve, place 2 pastry rolls on each plate. Top each roll with a poached egg. Pour 1/4 cup reserved Hollandaise Sauce over each egg.

Chef's Tips: Another well-known dish is Oysters Benedict, which calls for a single Egg Benedict surrounded by fried oysters.

**The ideal accompaniment for this brunch dish is freshly blanched jumbo asparagus or Broiled Tomatoes (page 141).**

## EGGS HUSSARD

Yield: 4 servings

*Chef's Note: Experimenting with Eggs Benedict, the Brennan family dreamed up this egg dish, which has enjoyed decades in the "Best of Brunch" category.*

2 cups Hollandaise Sauce (page 152)
1 cup Marchands de Vin Sauce (page 154)
8 Poached Eggs (page 79)
4 medium tomatoes
8 ounces Canadian bacon, thinly sliced
Salt and black pepper to taste
1 egg
1/2 cup whole milk
Vegetable oil for frying
1 cup all-purpose flour
1 cup dry bread crumbs

Prepare Hollandaise Sauce and Marchands de Vin Sauce; set aside and keep warm. Poach eggs; set aside. Warm bacon in skillet.

Cut tomatoes in half. Scoop out seeds, leaving tomato cups. Season tomatoes with salt and pepper. Mix egg and milk in a small bowl. Preheat oil to 350 degrees in deep fryer. Dredge tomatoes in flour, dip into egg wash and then dredge in bread crumbs. Fry tomato halves until crisp, about two minutes. Remove from oil, drain on a paper towel and reserve.

To serve: pour 1/4 cup reserved Marchands de Vin Sauce on each plate. Place 2 tomato halves in center of each plate; top each tomato with skillet-warmed bacon and a hot poached egg. Spoon 1/4 cup reserved Hollandaise Sauce on top of each egg.

Chef's Tip: If you don't want to deep-fry the tomatoes, try the recipe for Fried Green Tomatoes (page 48).

## EGGS MIGAS

Yield: 6 servings

*Chef's Note: When you live in the Southwest, you learn all about this scrambled egg dish because it is eaten from sunup to sundown. I prepare it by the skillet-full for a post-hunt breakfast on the ranch and consider it a necessary late night snack after an evening out.*

Pico de Gallo for garnish (page 153)
1 tablespoon vegetable oil or unsalted butter
1 pound andouille or spicy smoked sausage, cut into 1/8 inch thick slices

12 eggs, slightly beaten
Salt and black pepper to taste
6 tablespoons chopped tomato
3 tablespoons thinly sliced green onion
1 cup grated pepper Jack cheese
2 cups corn tortilla chips, broken into bite size pieces
Sour cream for garnish

Prepare Pico de Gallo; reserve. Heat oil in a large skillet over medium heat. Cook sausage until it begins to brown and fat is rendered. Add eggs, salt and pepper; stir. Fold in tomato, onion and cheese; cook until eggs are almost set. Toss in tortilla chips and cook mixture until set. To serve, garnish with reserved Pico de Gallo and sour cream.

Chef's Tips: In Texas we may make several substitutions to this dish, depending on what's available, like last night's left-over baked potatoes, steak or sausage.

We like to use blue corn chips for a special color contrast. Usually, we warm flour or corn tortillas to eat with this dish.

Egg Benedict and Egg Sardou = Eggs Brennan!

Texas Venison Hash with Fried Eggs

## TEXAS VENISON HASH WITH FRIED EGGS

Yield: 4 servings

*Chef's Note:  I grew up hunting Missouri white-tail deer, so when I moved south, I was happy to learn that Texas is also blessed with a very large white-tail deer population. Here is a tasty way to use smoked venison sausage — no matter what state it comes from! After an exhausting Sunday brunch employees revive with this comforting dish. One of our recipe testers said, "I do not like venison, but this was delicious."*

2 cups finely cubed potatoes
Creole Mustard Cream Sauce
   (page 32)
4 tablespoons vegetable oil, divided
1 cup (1/4-inch half moons) venison
   sausage
1/2 cup finely chopped yellow onion
1/4 cup finely chopped red bell
   pepper
1/4 cup finely chopped green bell
   pepper
2 tablespoons Louisiana
   hot pepper sauce
2 tablespoons Worcestershire sauce
Creole Meat Seasoning (page 156)
   to taste
Water as needed
4 eggs
2 tablespoons thinly sliced
   green onion

Cook potatoes just until tender; drain and reserve. Prepare Creole Mustard Cream Sauce; keep warm. Heat 2 tablespoons oil in a large skillet over medium-high heat. Add sausage, onion, red and green bell peppers; sauté 3 to 4 minutes, or until cooked through. Add reserved potatoes, hot sauce and Worcestershire; season to taste with meat seasoning. Pour in a small amount of water, if needed, to break up potatoes; stir until mixture is sticky. Remove from heat and cool in refrigerator, about 30 minutes. Preheat oven to 450 degrees. Form mixture into 4 (1-inch thick) oval-shaped cakes, or line the bottom of individual serving dishes with the mixture.

Heat remaining 2 tablespoons oil in a medium nonstick skillet over medium-high heat; sear cakes on both sides. Place cakes on a greased baking sheet; bake 5 to 7 minutes, or until heated through. Wipe nonstick skillet clean that was used for the hash cakes. Spray lightly with nonstick cooking spray. Fry eggs in same nonstick skillet. To serve, place a serving of hash in center of each plate, top with an egg and ladle reserved Creole Mustard Cream Sauce over top. Sprinkle with green onion to garnish.

Or bake hash in oven-proof dish and top with fried eggs.

Chef's Tips: Venison sausage can be found in some signature grocery stores. Or check the Source Guide. You can make the hash and the Creole Mustard Cream Sauce in advance and refrigerate until time to sear the hash and warm the sauce.

*"A gourmet who thinks of calories is like a tart who looks at her watch."*
*— James Beard*

## EGGS SARDOU

Yield: 4 servings

*Chef's Notes: Eggs Sardou (SAR-doo) was created in 1908 at Antoine's restaurant in tribute to French playwright Victorien Sardou. Traditionally, the dish combines Creamed Spinach, artichoke bottoms, and Poached Eggs, temptingly finished with Hollandaise Sauce. We take one Egg Sardou, pair it with one Egg Benedict, and entice our guests with a dynamic breakfast duo — Eggs Brennan.*

2 cups Hollandaise Sauce (page 152)
8 Poached Eggs (page 79)
2 cups Creamed Spinach (recipe follows)
8 artichoke bottoms, freshly cooked or canned

Prepare Hollandaise Sauce, Creamed Spinach and Poached Eggs; set aside and keep warm.

Place ½ cup reserved Creamed Spinach on each warmed plate and top with two warm artichoke bottoms.

Place a hot egg on each artichoke bottom and ladle ½ cup reserved Hollandaise Sauce over each serving of eggs. Serve immediately.

Chef's Tips: While writing this book, I was asked how to prepare Eggs Sardou for a large group. To do so, put the spinach into the bottom of a lightly greased glass or similar casserole dish. Top with artichoke bottoms; then add warm eggs. Finish heating in the oven until hot throughout; top with Hollandaise Sauce and a sprinkle of paprika.

## CREAMED SPINACH

Yield: 6 (½-cup) servings

2 (10-ounce) packages cleaned fresh spinach, divided
1 tablespoon vegetable oil, divided
½ cup finely chopped onion, divided
¾ cup whipping cream
1 (3-ounce) package cream cheese
Pinch of fresh-grated nutmeg
Splash of Pernod
Salt and black pepper to taste

Stem spinach and tear leaves.

Heat ½ tablespoon oil in a large skillet over medium-high heat; add ¼ cup onion and sauté until translucent. Stir in 10 ounces spinach and cook about 2 minutes, stirring frequently. Remove spinach; set aside.

Repeat previous steps with remaining ½ tablespoon oil, ¼ cup onion, and 10 ounces spinach.

Lower heat to medium and add first batch of sautéed spinach to skillet.

Heat cream and cream cheese in a small saucepan over low heat until cream cheese melts into cream. Stir into spinach and cook until heated through.

Season with nutmeg, Pernod, salt and pepper before serving.

## AUNT ADELAIDE'S KITCHEN

Our new kitchen allows us the space to do comfortably what we'd been doing — cramped — for 30 years. Nonetheless, it's a tribute to Alex's Aunt Adelaide Brennan's dream kitchen in New Orleans. She owned a Garden District home which she restored over three decades (the kitchen was first of course.) Alex borrowed his Aunt's "cherub" motif for the Brennan's of Houston kitchen. And you'll notice those same plump cherubs frolicking on our menu and this cookbook cover. Above our main line, cherubs busily make gumbo; others cavort around the kitchen's perimeter. Certainly, the restaurant kitchen is functional, but Alex succeeded in imparting the welcoming, nurturing feeling he felt in Aunt Adelaide's New Orleans kitchen.

## OYSTER CAKES AND EGGS

Yield: 4 servings

*Chef's Note: Being on the Gulf Coast certainly has its advantages when it comes to fresh, fresh seafood. Since there are good oysters found on other seaboards, savor these oyster cakes no matter where you'll be consuming them.*

1 cup Hollandaise Sauce
   (page 152)
3 cups Creole Oyster Stuffing
   (page 143)
2 tablespoons vegetable oil
4 Poached Eggs (page 79)
Vegetable oil for deep frying
1 tablespoon Creole Seafood
   Seasoning, (page 157) divided
2/3 cup all-purpose flour
1/3 cup corn meal or masa harina
24 fresh oysters, shucked

Prepare Hollandaise Sauce; reserve until needed.
   Prepare and bake Creole Oyster Stuffing according to recipe.
   Preheat oven to 350 degrees.
   Form baked stuffing into 4 cakes. Heat 2 tablespoons oil in medium skillet over medium-high heat; sear cakes on each side until lightly browned. Place cakes on a greased baking sheet. Heat cakes in oven 8 to10 minutes, or until hot throughout; reserve and keep warm until ready to use.
   Prepare Poached Eggs; reserve until needed.
   Heat oil in deep fryer to 350 degrees.
   Combine 1/2 tablespoon Creole Seafood Seasoning, flour and corn meal in a small bowl. Dredge oysters in flour mixture and deep fry until crisp. Drain

oysters on a paper towel; season with remaining 1/2 tablespoon Creole Seafood Seasoning and reserve.
   Reheat Poached Eggs.
   To serve, place a warm oyster cake in center of each plate, top with an egg, drizzle with reserved Hollandaise Sauce and surround with 6 fried oysters.

Chef's Tip: When buying fresh shucked oysters, look for a date on the container. We recommend using oysters within a week of the packaging date. There are several Internet sites that offer fresh seafood. For crisper oysters, fry in small batches.

## LOUISIANA CRAWFISH AND EGGS

Yield: 4 servings

*Chef's Note: Crawfish lends itself to an endless variety of crowd-pleasing preparations. Customers give the thumbs up to our crawfish cakes, which we embellish with poached eggs and a buttery sauté of crawfish for a double dose of goodness.*

8 Poached Eggs (page 79)
1 tablespoon oil
3/4 cup finely chopped onion
3/4 cup finely chopped green bell
   pepper
1/4 cup finely chopped celery
2 teaspoons minced garlic
1 pound crawfish tail meat
1 teaspoon Louisiana hot
   pepper sauce
2 teaspoons Creole Seafood
   Seasoning (page 157)
1 tablespoon Worcestershire sauce

Inviting courtyard at Brennan's of Houston

2 tablespoons grated Parmesan
  cheese
1 egg
¼ cup dry bread crumbs
2 tablespoons thinly sliced
  green onion
1 cup milk
2 eggs
½ cup all-purpose flour
Dry bread crumbs as needed
  for dredging
Vegetable oil for frying
1 recipe Sautéed Crawfish Sauce
  (page 151)

Prepare Poached Eggs; reserve until needed.

Heat oil in a medium skillet over medium-high heat. Add onion, bell pepper, celery and garlic; sauté until translucent. Reduce heat to medium; add crawfish, hot sauce, Creole Seafood Seasoning, Worcestershire and cheese to vegetables and cook until heated through.

Remove skillet from heat. Stir in 1 slightly beaten egg, ¼ cup bread crumbs and green onion; form mixture into 8 cakes. Combine remaining 2 eggs and milk in a small bowl for egg wash. Dust crawfish cakes with flour, dip into egg wash and dredge in bread crumbs.

Heat oil in a large skillet over medium-high heat. Add crawfish cakes and sauté until golden-brown and heated through; drain on paper towel. Keep warm in oven.

Prepare Sautéed Crawfish Sauce.

To serve, place 2 crawfish cakes on each plate, top each cake with a reheated poached egg and ¼ cup crawfish sauce.

Chef's Tips: Since crawfish may not be the easiest thing to come by in some places, check the Source Guide (page 186) for advice on locating terrific ingredients. Crawfish season generally runs from early January through June and at the season's end, they sometimes lose some of their sweetness — add a splash of brandy to sweeten. Frozen Asian crawfish are available year-round. Andouille sausage is an optional ingredient in Sautéed Crawfish Sauce for this recipe.

*"The discovery of a new dish does more for the happiness of mankind than the discovery of a new star."*

*— A. Brillat Savarin*

78

Yvonne Washington and her jazz quartet

## POACHED EGGS

Yield: 6 servings

*Chef's Note: I'm sure that we've poached over a million eggs. Company-wide, the total eggs poached would number in the multi-millions. In other words, we have it down pat by now! Poaching eggs is a vital technique to have in your cooking repertoire.*

1 gallon water
3/4 cup distilled vinegar
12 eggs

Combine water and vinegar in a large stockpot over medium-high heat; bring to a simmer.

Break each egg into a cup and then carefully slide egg into poaching water.

Cook about 3 minutes, or until whites are set and opaque.

Remove eggs from water with slotted spoon; blot with towel and use immediately.

If reserving eggs for later use, place in shallow pan filled with ice water.

When ready to serve, reheat in hot water and use.

Chef's Tips: Follow this simple recipe. Do not put any salt in the water during poaching or the eggs will fall apart.

To have a backup in case of last minute egg breakage, I like to poach an extra egg or two when preparing a recipe.

## SOFT-SHELL CRABS AND EGGS

Yield: 6 servings

*Chef's Note: Our soft-shell crabs have to pass the "tickle" test. If they're not lively, we don't want them. Soft-shell crabs are specialties in spring and fall, when blue crabs molt, shedding their hard outer shell, before growing another. At the restaurant, we offer fried soft-shell crabs with Choron Sauce as a luncheon or dinner entrée.*

2 cups Choron Sauce (page 153)
6 Poached Eggs (page 79)
6 tablespoons jumbo lump crabmeat, cleaned and picked over
Creole Seafood Seasoning
   (page 157) as needed
1 teaspoon mayonnaise
1/2 teaspoon Creole mustard
6 cups vegetable oil
6 soft-shell crabs, cleaned
2 cups all-purpose flour
2 eggs
1 cup milk
3 cups bread crumbs

Prepare Choron Sauce; reserve until needed. Prepare Poached Eggs; reserve.

Combine crabmeat, 1/4 teaspoon seafood seasoning, mayonnaise and mustard in a small bowl. Gently stuff tail end of crab cavities with crabmeat mixture. Heat oil to 325 degrees in deep fryer. Season crabs with 1 tablespoon seafood seasoning. Dredge in flour. Combine eggs and milk in a small bowl; dip crabs into egg wash. Dredge crabs in bread

crumbs. Fry crabs until crisp and drain on a paper towel.

Reheat reserved Poached Eggs. To serve, place a crab in center of each plate and top with an egg. Ladle reserved Choron Sauce over all.

Chef's Tip: Have the seafood market clean soft shell crabs when purchasing, or to clean the crabs yourself, lift each side of the shell and gently remove gills at the base of the crab. Pull off the tail at the base — wide tails are girls, skinny tails are boys. Remove the face — the eyes and little area around the mouth. Since fresh soft-shells aren't always available, you can purchase them frozen.

*"Red bean & ricely yours."*
*— Louis Armstrong*

## BERRY, BERRY PARFAIT

Yield: 6 servings

*Chef's Note: This towering medley of mascarpone, berries and Homemade Granola makes for a soothing, delicious way to greet the day.*

Homemade Granola (recipe follows)
Warm Mascarpone Cream Sauce
   (recipe follows)
Sweetened Whipped Cream
   (recipe follows)
2 cups fresh mixed berries
   (raspberries, blueberries, blackberries or a combination)

Prepare Homemade Granola; reserve. Prepare Warm Mascarpone Sauce; reserve, keeping warm. Prepare Sweetened Whipped Cream; reserve.

Place 2 tablespoons Mascarpone Sauce in each parfait or wine glass. Add layers of Homemade Granola and berries. Repeat layers and top with generous dollop of whipped cream and sprinkle with granola.

## HOMEMADE GRANOLA

1/2 cup quick oats
1 tablespoon unsalted butter
1/2 cup sliced almonds, unsalted
1/2 cup pecan pieces
1/2 cup golden raisins
3/4 cup packed brown sugar

Berry, Berry Parfait;
Oatmeal and Berry Custard

Lightly brown oats in butter in a medium skillet over medium-high heat. Add almonds, pecans, raisins and sugar to skillet; stir constantly until sugar begins to melt. Reserve until needed.

## SWEETENED WHIPPED CREAM

1/3 cup whipping cream
2 teaspoons sugar
1/4 teaspoon vanilla extract

Whip cream, sugar and vanilla in a small bowl until stiff peaks form.

## WARM MASCARPONE SAUCE

1 1/2 cups whipping cream
6 tablespoons sugar
3/4 cup mascarpone cheese
3 egg yolks
2 to 3 tablespoons Grand Marnier
   or vanilla extract

In a medium saucepan, bring cream and sugar to a simmer over medium heat until sugar is dissolved. Add mascarpone; mix until incorporated with cream and heated through. Place yolks in a small bowl. Temper yolks with hot cream mixture by first stirring a small amount of the cream mixture into yolks, then slowly add tempered yolks into remaining cream mixture. Be careful not to let this sauce come to a boil — the sauce would curdle. Strain sauce and stir in Grand Marnier. Serve warm.

## OATMEAL AND BERRY CUSTARD

Yield: 8 servings

*Chef's Note: Oatmeal isn't one of Alex Brennan-Martin's pet dishes, but it was hard for him to argue with the impassioned raves from our guests about this dish. Oatmeal and Berry Custard has always been one of our most-requested brunch recipes.*

5 eggs, beaten
1 1/2 cups milk
3/4 cup whipping cream
1 cup plus 2 tablespoons packed
   brown sugar
1 teaspoon cinnamon
2 1/2 cups cooked oatmeal, cooled
1/2 teaspoon vanilla extract
1 1/2 cups fresh berries (raspberries,
   blueberries, blackberries or a
   mixture of berries), divided
Sweetened Whipped Cream
   for garnish

Preheat oven to 350 degrees. Mix eggs, milk and cream in a medium bowl. Strain mixture into a large bowl, fully incorporating egg into mixture; discard any residue. Combine sugar and cinnamon in a small bowl. Add sugar-cinnamon, oatmeal and vanilla to egg mixture. Stir lightly until mixed.

Lightly butter 8 (1-cup) ramekins. Divide 1 cup berries among ramekins; fill with custard to within 1/4 inch of top; set into a baking pan. Fill baking pan with water that comes three-fourths up the sides of ramekins. Cover entire pan with foil and bake 1 hour, or until custard is firm. Remove ramekins from water bath.

Serve warm, garnished with a dollop of whipped cream and remaining 1/2 cup berries.

Baked D'Anjou Pears

## BAKED D'ANJOU PEARS

Yield: 4 servings

*Chef's Note: Consider this a "pear-fect" way to start your day — especially since the Pears, Homemade Granola, and Warm Mascarpone Cream Sauce can be prepared the day before.*

¼ cup Homemade Granola
  (page 81)
4 D'Anjou pears
1 teaspoon whole cloves
1 stick cinnamon
2 cups packed brown sugar
2 cups inexpensive port wine
1½ cups Warm Mascarpone
  Cream Sauce (page 81)
8 sprigs of mint

Prepare Homemade Granola; reserve. Preheat oven to 325 degrees.

Slice pears in half lengthwise and remove seeds, but do not peel. Cut lengthwise slits every ¼ inch into pear halves beginning 1 inch from top of pear so that a fan forms when pear half is cooked.

Place pears, cloves and cinnamon stick in a deep 2-quart baking dish. Sprinkle tops of pears with sugar, and pour wine over pears. Cover dish with aluminum foil and bake 45 to 60 minutes, or until a knife inserted in pear comes out easily.

Prepare Warm Mascarpone Sauce; reserve, keeping warm. Remove pears from baking dish and drain on paper towels. Pat slightly with paper towel to eliminate excess liquid. For presentation, ladle reserved Warm Mascarpone Sauce on each plate, place 1 pear fan over sauce, and sprinkle Homemade Granola around the pear and over sauce. Finish with a sprig of mint.

Chef's Tips: Besides D'Anjou pears, feel free to select Red Bartlett or Bosc pears.

Use a pancake turner to lift pear fans from baking dish to help keep the fan shape open.

Adelaide and Alexandra Brennan-Martin, 4th generation Brennan family, cooking at Brennan's

Tish Strangmeyer photography

I want every recipe to be successful, and the team working on this cookbook has intensively tested all the recipes we offer. The sous chefs and I started the testing process by breaking our recipes down into small quantities. The recipes would then go to our host of food testers — ranging from staff, their families and other friends. We would take their notes and often re-work the recipes based on those comments. What's more, I hired three women who are home cooks to test recipes on a home range that I had installed in the main kitchen. I worked with them as they tested the recipes again. They always say a chef is happiest when he's cooking — it's certainly been fun testing these recipes for this book.

As you can imagine, our beef, pork, venison, veal and poultry dishes take on a New Orleans edge as they wind their way through and out of our kitchen. Whether it's the Creole mustard used to pack extra flavor into an accompanying sauce or Brennan's of Houston's own rendition of a Creole Meat Seasoning used on all types of entrées, one bite and you'll know we stake our reputation on our main dish offerings.

Too, it's important to recognize that the demi-glacés we use at Brennan's of Houston — and so important to our cuisine — easily can be replicated in your kitchen — and make a difference in the quality of your meal. In this section, we discuss ways to prepare and present — and easy substitutions to assist the everyday cook.

chef carl
recommends

Chicken Pontalba

## THE GHOSTS OF THE JUNIOR LEAGUE PAST

Our building, designed in 1930 by noted Houston, Texas architect John Staub, was more known for teas and ladies' meetings than New Orleans-style dining because it originally housed the Junior League of Houston. When we came to Houston in 1967, it was obvious this Creole-style building was meant for us. Today, many who remember attending Junior League dances love to peek in the ballroom and remember those happy times. We respect this building's history and value the atmosphere that contributes to our dining experience.

## CHEF CARL'S PEPPERCORN-CRUSTED FILET MIGNON

Yield: 4 servings

*Chef's Note: This is high on our list of winning recipes and is well worth the effort to make the accompanying Au Poivre Sauce. As stellar pairings, I recommend serving the Filet Mignon with one of the following: Vegetable Hash (page 146), Gorgonzola Walnut Mashed Potatoes (page 136) or Texas Cornbread Pudding (page 143).*

1 cup Au Poivre Sauce (page 87)
4 (8-ounce) beef tenderloin filets
1/2 tablespoon Creole Meat
    Seasoning (page 156)
1/4 cup mixed or black peppercorns,
    crushed or coarsely ground
2 tablespoons vegetable oil
4 (1/4-inch thick) onion slices

Prepare Au Poivre Sauce; reserve, keeping warm until needed. Preheat oven to 400 degrees. Season filets with Creole Meat Seasoning; press pepper into both sides to form crust. Heat oil in an ovenproof medium skillet over medium-high heat; sear meat on both sides.

Place onion slices on baking sheet and top each with a filet. Finish in oven to desired doneness. Or, if desired, grill meat over hot coals on barbecue to desired doneness. Serve with reserved Au Poivre Sauce. Garnish with roasted onion slices.

Chef's Tips:  A good iron skillet is priceless for cooking the steaks. Chefs go by feel when it comes to checking the doneness of steaks; the firmer the meat the more done it is. If you don't want to chance it by feel, there are a number of meat thermometers available; I prefer the digital ones. When using a thermometer, try to insert it into the center of the meat. Whenever cooking meat or poultry in the oven, I like to place them on onion slices or some mirepoix, a mixture of sautéed onion, carrots, celery and herbs. This protects the bottom of the meat or poultry from becoming dry or tough and yields mighty tasty vegetables.

Substitute T-bone or rib-eye steaks for the filet of beef. If doing so, go lighter on the peppercorns.

*"Life is short, eat well!"*
*— Alex Brennan-Martin*

## AU POIVRE SAUCE

Yield: 1 cup

1 cup Veal or Beef Demi-Glacé
   (page 69)
1 teaspoon vegetable oil
2 shallots, minced
1/4 cup red wine
1/4 cup brandy
1 tablespoon green peppercorns,
   rinsed
1/4 cup whipping cream
Salt and black pepper to taste

Prepare Veal or Beef Demi-Glacé; reserve, keeping warm until needed. Heat oil in a medium skillet over medium heat; add shallots and cook until translucent. Add wine, brandy and peppercorns. BE CAREFUL of a possible flame up when adding brandy. Reduce heat and simmer until reduced by half.

Add reserved Veal Demi-Glacé; reduce again until thick enough to coat the back of spoon. Stir in cream; simmer 2 to 3 minutes. Add salt and pepper, adjusting seasonings as needed. Sauce may be stored in a covered container in refrigerator up to 1 week.

Chef's Tip: Another version of the basic Au Poivre is Raisin Peppercorn Sauce. For grilled meats such as beef and veal, it's a "don't miss" way to go. Soak 1/3 cup golden or dark raisins in 1/4 cup red port wine 30 minutes. In place of red wine, add the macerated raisin-port mixture.

Chef Carl's Peppercorn-Crusted Filet Mignon on Vegetable Hash

# BEEF WELLINGTON CREOLE-STYLE

Yield: 6 to 8 servings

*Chef's Note: The French took a fancy to filet de boeuf en croute (filet of beef in pastry) for banquet fare in the early 19th century. As an accolade to the English hero of the Battle of Waterloo, this classic filet took on his name. The entrée showpiece was indeed a particular favorite of the Duke of Wellington. Here in the 21st century, to impart a Creole edge, I replaced the mushroom duxelle filling of former times with Our Creole Oyster Stuffing. Steamed asparagus and Maple-Glazed Carrots with Rosemary (page 140) are a colorful accompaniment to this grand entrée. Making Beef Wellington Creole-Style for the holidays will assure you of the undying devotion of family and friends.*

1 recipe Creole Oyster Stuffing (page 143)
¼ cup vegetable oil, divided
1 (2- to 3-pound) center cut beef tenderloin (5 to 6 ounces per person)
Creole Meat Seasoning (page 156)
½ cup prepared pâté, optional
2 to 3 packages puff pastry dough — NOT phyllo dough
½ cup dry, plain bread crumbs
1 egg
2 tablespoons water
1 recipe Béarnaise Sauce (page 153)

Prepare Creole Oyster Stuffing and bake; reserve covered in refrigerator until needed. May be done day before.

Preheat oven to 350 degrees.

Lightly oil and season tenderloin with Creole Meat Seasoning.

Heat remaining oil in very hot skillet or roasting pan; sear meat on all sides.

After searing, transfer tenderloin to oven and roast uncovered until internal temperature reaches 115 degrees.

Remove tenderloin from oven; cover and refrigerate until chilled. May be done day before.

Morning of serving day — make a lengthwise incision in chilled tenderloin along middle of top from end to end, about 1¼ inches deep.

Soften pâté by working it with a spoon; rub entire tenderloin with a thin coating of pâté, avoiding the cut along top.

Open cut on top and fill with Creole Oyster Stuffing.

On a sheet of parchment paper, lay out 1 sheet of puff pastry dough.

Sprinkle bread crumbs in center of dough where meat will be placed.

With Oyster Stuffing facing up, place meat on top of bread crumbs.

Combine egg and water to make egg wash; brush on pastry all the way around the meat.

Lay remaining sheet of pastry on top of tenderloin and press down around the meat. Trim pastry, leaving a 1½-inch border around meat. Using a fork, seal pastry all the way around the tenderloin. (Save leftover pastry scraps to decorate top.)

Follow directions in Chef's Tip below to create decoration of choice for top of Wellington. Brush remaining egg wash on top and refrigerate tenderloin, covered with plastic wrap, until ready to bake.

Just before baking Wellington, prepare Béarnaise Sauce; reserve, keeping warm.

Preheat oven to 350 degrees. Bake Wellington until desired doneness is reached; check using a digital stem meat thermometer: 130° rare, 140° medium-rare, 160° medium, and 170° to 180° for medium-well to well-done.

Let Wellington rest 10 to 15 minutes before slicing with a long, sharp serrated knife. Arrange on meat platter and accompany with reserved Béarnaise Sauce.

Chef's Tip: Locate puff pastry dough—NOT phyllo dough—packaged in a long rectangular box, in your grocery's frozen food section. You will need puff pastry both to cover the beef and to garnish it, so buy an extra box of dough for decorations. Follow thawing instructions on the box. In advance, I find it especially handy to lay the pastry out flat on a parchment paper-lined sheet pan, cover with plastic wrap, and refreeze.

To prepare Wellington, thaw dough and lay it out flat according to above directions. Place in freezer long enough to get firm. Ideally, one sheet will cover the bottom of the Wellington and a second one the top. If Wellington is longer than the pastry, combine two sheets of pastry for bottom by egg washing the ends and pressing down on edges to form a tight seal. Do the same for the top cover.

Once beef is encased in pastry, my first decorating choice is to make braids with extra dough. Cut another sheet of dough lengthwise into 3 strips ¼ inch wide, leaving the 3 strips connected at one end. Make two braids. Braid the 3 strips by carefully laying the right strip over the center strip. Then place the left strip over the center one. Repeat crisscrossing all the way to the end. Brush the Wellington with egg wash. Crisscross braids over the Wellington from corner to corner, forming an "X" on top. Press down corners of braids and trim any excess.

A second special touch is to use cookie cutters to make desired designs and afix them to the egg-washed Wellington. Then egg-wash the cutouts for a golden finish.

Determining the desired doneness is one of the hardest steps in preparing this recipe. A digital stem meat thermometer is vital for checking the internal temperature of the meat. Insert the thermometer between the braids, aiming for the center of the meat, to obtain the most accurate reading.

## BEEF TIPS DIANE

Yield: 4 servings

*Chef's Note: Beef Tips Diane is the hungry man's pick for a nourishing winter lunch. If you're a steak-and-potatoes kind of diner, go big time for this one.*

1 1/2 pounds beef tenderloin,
   cut into 1-inch cubes
2 teaspoons Creole Meat Seasoning
   (page 156)
1/4 cup vegetable oil
16 pearl onions, peeled and
   blanched until tender
1 teaspoon minced garlic
8 ounces wild mushrooms (such as
   shiitake, oyster or cremini), sliced
1/2 cup red wine
1 cup Beef or Veal Demi-Glacé
   (page 69)
1/4 cup cold unsalted butter, cubed
Salt and black pepper to taste
2 tablespoons thinly sliced
   green onion

Beef Tips Diane

Season beef with Creole Meat Seasoning.

Heat oil in a large skillet over medium-high heat; add beef tips and sear 1 to 2 minutes to get a nice brown color; remove from pan and set aside.

Add pearl onions to skillet; sauté 3 to 5 minutes, letting meat juices evaporate and onions caramelize.

Stir in garlic and cook 30 seconds; then add mushrooms and sauté 2 minutes.

Reduce heat to medium, add wine, and cook until liquid is reduced by half.

Add Demi-Glacé and reserved beef tips to skillet; cook until meat reaches desired doneness.

Slowly add butter, whisking after each addition.

Season with salt and pepper; sprinkle with green onion.

Chef's Tips: Professional chefs finish a sauce by swirling butter into the sauce over the heat — without using a whisk. If you go for the "swirl" method, be sure to avoid swirling the sauce on yourself!

Serve over mashed potatoes, couscous, rice or pasta of choice.

## BRAISED VENISON SHANKS AND BLACK-EYED PEA CASSOULET

Yield: 6 servings

*Chef's Note: Being a hunter and a chef, I enjoy processing my own game. I usually process it to have the same cuts of meat that we buy for the restaurant. Many times hunters use the shanks only for sausage-making. I think shanks are among the most flavorful cuts. I always remove the smaller fore and larger hind shanks at the knee and then French the small end of the bone by cutting about 1 to 1 1/2 inches of meat away from the bone, exposing a nice clean bone end.*

90

6 venison shanks
6 tablespoons Creole Meat
    Seasoning (page 156)
2 cups all-purpose flour
1/2 cup vegetable oil
I cup chopped onion
1/2 cup chopped carrot
1/2 cup chopped celery
6 whole cloves garlic
1/2 cup chopped canned tomatoes
I tablespoon orange zest
I orange, juice of
2 sprigs fresh thyme
2 sprigs fresh oregano
3 bay leaves
6 cups Venison, Beef or Veal Stock
    (page 69)
1 1/3 cups red wine
I tablespoon cornstarch
    (if needed)
I tablespoon cold water
    (if needed)
2 tablespoons butter
2 cups fully cooked
    black-eyed peas
1/2 cup chopped turnip, blanched
1/2 cup chopped carrot, blanched
1/2 cup chopped rutabaga, blanched
Salt and black pepper to taste

Preheat oven to 325 degrees. Season venison with Creole Meat Seasoning, rubbing in well. Coat evenly with flour. Heat oil in a 12- or 14-inch cast iron skillet or heavy roasting pan over medium heat. Add venison and sear on all sides; remove meat from pan and reserve.

Add onion, carrot, celery and garlic to pan and sauté until vegetables start to caramelize. Return meat to pan; add tomatoes, orange zest, juice from orange, thyme, oregano, bay leaves, stock and wine. Cover with foil and place in oven 2 hours, or until meat is tender. Meat should be almost ready to fall off the bone when done.

Remove meat from pan and keep warm.

Strain liquid into a medium saucepan and skim fat off top. Simmer over medium heat, skimming occasionally until liquid reduces to yield about 2 cups. If liquid doesn't reduce to medium consistency, combine cornstarch and cold water and add slowly to simmering sauce, until sauce starts to coat the back of a spoon. Set aside.

Heat butter in a medium skillet over medium-high heat. Add black-eyed peas, turnip, carrot and rutabaga; sauté 3 to 5 minutes. Add sautéed vegetables to sauce; simmer 3 to 5 minutes. Season cassoulet sauce with salt and pepper. To serve, ladle sauce over venison shanks.

Chef's Tips:  If you don't have venison, check the Source Guide, page 186. Or substitute lamb shanks or veal osso buco for the venison shanks, following the same cooking steps.

You can substitute canned beef broth for the stock. I prefer brands that don't contain salt or MSG.

Serve with one of your favorite flavor Potato Smashers (pages 136 – 139).

Braised Venison Shanks and Black-Eyed Pea Cassoulet

Panéed Veal and Shrimp

## PANÉED VEAL
## AND SHRIMP

Yield: 4 servings

*Chef's Note: If you can't decide whether to serve your guests meat or seafood, serve this and double their culinary pleasure with shrimp fettuccine laced with Lemon Vermouth Cream and accented with the veal. Vive la différence!*

Lemon Vermouth Cream
  (recipe follows)
8 (1 1/2-ounce) veal flank slices or
  veal escallops
1/4 cup milk
2 eggs
2 cups unseasoned dry bread
  crumbs
Zest of 2 lemons
1 tablespoon Creole Meat
  Seasoning
1 cup all-purpose flour
Vegetable oil as needed

3 quarts water
1 tablespoon salt
12 ounces dry fettuccine
1 pound (36/42 count) shrimp,
  peeled and deveined
1 tablespoon Creole Seafood
  Seasoning (page 157)
1/2 cup thinly sliced green onion
Salt and black pepper to taste

Prepare Lemon Vermouth
Cream; reserve, keeping warm.

Place veal between 2 sheets of plastic wrap; pound to ⅛-inch thickness. In small bowl or flat-bottom container, whisk milk and eggs for egg wash. In another small bowl or flat-bottom container, combine bread crumbs and lemon zest. Season both sides of veal with Creole Meat Seasoning. Dredge in flour, dip into egg wash and then into bread crumb mixture, pressing crumbs onto meat.

Heat ¼ cup oil in a large skillet over medium-high heat. Sear several pieces of veal 2 minutes on each side, or until cooked through; reserve, keeping warm. If skillet gets crusted with breadcrumbs, wipe skillet clean. Heat another ¼ cup oil and repeat procedure until all veal is cooked.

Bring water to a boil in a large stockpot; stir in salt. Add fettuccine to boiling water and cook a little less than "al dente," about 7 to 8 minutes; drain pasta thoroughly but do not rinse. While pasta is cooking, heat 2 tablespoons oil in a large skillet over medium-high heat. Add shrimp and Creole Seafood Seasoning; sauté 2 to 3 minutes, or until shrimp are cooked through.

Combine freshly cooked pasta, reserved Lemon Vermouth Cream and green onion. Toss together and adjust seasoning with salt and pepper.

To serve, divide pasta among 4 plates. Arrange veal slices and shrimp around pasta. Serve immediately.

**Chef's Tips:** Consider substituting 4 boneless, skinless whole chicken breasts pounded to ¼-inch thickness.

If the pasta mixture becomes too thick, thin it out with a little water or a touch more whipping cream.

Always remember to cook pasta just to "al dente" (slight resistance to the tooth).

## LEMON VERMOUTH CREAM

Yield: 1½ cups

*Chef's Note: Lemon Vermouth Cream delights appreciative diners, especially when teamed with Panéed Veal and Shrimp.*

1 tablespoon vegetable oil
⅓ cup chopped shallots
1 lemon, peeled and sliced
1 teaspoon black peppercorns
1 bay leaf
1 cup vermouth
2 cups whipping cream
Salt and white pepper to taste

Heat oil in a small saucepan over medium-high heat; add shallots and cook until translucent. Add lemon, peppercorns, bay leaf and vermouth; bring to a boil. Reduce heat and simmer to reduce liquid until almost syrupy.

Add cream and cook over medium heat to reduce mixture until just thick enough to coat the back of a spoon. Strain through a fine mesh strainer; season with salt and pepper. Reserve, keeping warm until needed.

**Chef's Tip:** Use a little splash of water to rinse the final cream out of the pan when straining the sauce. This allows the mixture to go through the strainer more easily.

## Veal Rib-Eye with Artichokes and Mushrooms

Yield: 6 servings

*Chef's Note: When certain guests see any dish on our menu with artichokes and mushrooms like these tender slices of veal rib-eye nestled in an aromatic crust, they automatically order it!*

1/2 cup Creole mustard
2 tablespoons minced shallots
1 tablespoon minced garlic
1 teaspoon finely chopped
  fresh basil
1 teaspoon finely chopped
  fresh oregano
1 teaspoon finely chopped
  fresh thyme
1 (2 1/4-pound) veal rib-eye
1 1/2 tablespoons Creole
  Meat Seasoning (page 156)
1/4 cup vegetable oil, divided
1 recipe Sun-Dried Tomato and
  Basil Beurre Blanc (page 155)
6 artichoke hearts (fresh, canned
  or marinated)
2 cups sliced mushrooms (any combination, such as shiitake, oyster
  or button mushrooms)
Salt and black pepper to taste

Preheat oven to 350 degrees. In a medium bowl combine mustard, shallots, garlic, basil, oregano and thyme; reserve until needed for crust. Rub rib-eye with Creole Meat Seasoning. Heat 2 tablespoons oil in a large skillet over medium-high heat; sear rib-eye on all sides, about 1 to 2 minutes per side. Place skillet (if ovenproof; otherwise transfer meat to roasting pan) in oven and roast meat about 20 to 30 minutes, or until internal temperature is 105 degrees when tested with a digital stem meat thermometer. Place veal in refrigerator to cool 10 to 20 minutes. Rub reserved crust mixture over entire cooled rib-eye. Roast may be prepared up to this point in the morning the day of serving.

Place meat on a wire rack in a medium roasting pan in preheated 350-degree oven 30 to 45 minutes, or until internal temperature reaches 145 to 155 degrees for medium doneness. While meat is roasting, prepare Sun-Dried Tomato and Basil Beurre Blanc; reserve, keeping warm. Remove meat from oven and cover loosely with aluminum foil for 10 minutes to allow juices to be reabsorbed into the meat.

Heat remaining 2 tablespoons oil in a medium skillet over medium-high heat. Add artichoke hearts and mushrooms; sauté 3 minutes, or until tender. Season with salt and pepper; reserve, keeping warm. To serve, slice veal into 12 thin slices and top with reserved artichoke-mushroom sauté; finish with reserved Sun-Dried Tomato and Basil Beurre Blanc.

Chef's Tip: Use artichokes, mushrooms and the same Beurre Blanc for toppings to vary this entrée with sautéed veal cutlets. Or, substitute a pork loin roast for the rib-eye. Sear and roast the pork loin following veal directions. If you like a little pink left showing in the meat, roast pork to internal temperature of 160 degrees. Veal, however, is a meat that I was taught to cook to medium doneness.

*"If you can organize your kitchen, you can arrange your life."*
— Louis Parrish

Veal Rib-Eye with Artichokes
and Mushrooms

## VEAL CHOP TCHOUPITOULAS

Yield: 6 servings

*Chef's Note: Whenever we take this signature classic off the menu, it doesn't stop our guests from ordering it! The Tchoupitoulas Sauce makes this delectable entrée one you'll relish preparing for your guests. North of New Orleans, river-dwelling Indians called the Tchoupitoulas (Chop-ah-TOO-las) began trading with the first settlers. One of their gifts to the New Orleans area was the spectacular costumes associated with Mardi Gras. This spectacular meat sauce can dress up a meal for you, too!*

1 cup Tchoupitoulas Sauce (recipe follows)
1 tablespoon green peppercorns, rinsed
1 tablespoon finely chopped pimiento
6 (10- to 12-ounce) veal chops
2 tablespoons vegetable oil
1½ tablespoons Creole Meat Seasoning (page 156)

If grilling veal chops, light coals. Or, if finishing in oven, preheat to 400 degrees. Prepare Tchoupitoulas Sauce; reserve, keeping warm until needed.

Combine peppercorns and pimiento in a small custard cup; reserve until needed. Rub chops with oil and season with Creole Meat Seasoning. Grill chops over hot coals until desired doneness. Or, sear chops in a large cast iron skillet over medium-high heat. Transfer skillet to oven to finish cooking to desired doneness.

To serve, top each chop with a scant 3 tablespoons Tchoupitoulas Sauce; garnish top of each chop with 1 teaspoon reserved peppercorn and pimiento mixture.

Chef's Tip: If you're inviting friends over, be sure to serve these chops with a heaping helping of Texas Cornbread Pudding (page 143) on the side. For a special occasion, I prefer a topping of a rich Sautéed Crawfish Sauce (page 151). Beef or another meat is also a solid option for the veal chops.

## TCHOUPITOULAS SAUCE

Yield: 1 cup

*Chef's Note: Not only does this sauce carry the name of the influential Louisianan Indian tribe near the Crescent City, Tchoupitoulas is also a well-known street in New Orleans proper. This powerful sauce is a long-standing staple. Regularly used to dress Veal Chop Tchoupitoulas, this particular glaze would make most meats, including chicken, mighty proud. You will taste the richness of the port followed by flavors ranging from the sweetness of the honey to the tartness of the vinegar, the light herb flavor of the rosemary to the zing of the peppercorns. We like to garnish the sauce with finely chopped roasted red bell pepper or pimiento and green peppercorns as a final touch.*

2 teaspoons vegetable oil
1 teaspoon minced shallots
1 teaspoon minced garlic
2 tablespoons brandy
½ cup Veal or Beef Demi-Glacé (page 157)
¼ cup port wine
3 tablespoons honey
3 tablespoons red wine vinegar
1 tablespoon chopped fresh rosemary leaves
2 tablespoons finely chopped pimientos
2 tablespoons green peppercorns, rinsed under water
1 tablespoon unsalted butter, softened

Heat oil in a small saucepan; add shallots and garlic. Sauté 1 minute to bring out the flavor. De-glaze pan with brandy, being very watchful to avoid any flames the brandy might ignite.

Or, pull pan off to side and let cool a few minutes. Then add brandy and swish around with spoon or whisk to de-glaze. Add Veal Demi-Glacé, wine, honey and vinegar. Reduce liquid about 3 to 5 minutes, or until it coats the back of a spoon. Add rosemary, letting sauce steep, off the heat, about 5 minutes.

Strain sauce through a fine mesh strainer. Add pimientos and green peppercorns. Finish with butter, by whisking small pieces into warm sauce while rotating saucepan on and off low heat. Serve immediately.

## ROASTED PORK TENDERLOIN WITH SPICY FIG SAUCE

Yield: 6 servings

*Chef's Note: Finish grilled pork tenderloins with a delicious Spicy Fig Sauce and serve with our Vegetable Hash, a medley of flavorful vegetables. The Fig Sauce compliments venison back-strap or other tender cuts of venison or elk. In Missouri, I prepared this entrée on a charcoal grill in November for my mother and her friends at their "Aunts' Party," which is what they call their group.*

1½ cups Spicy Fig Sauce
  (recipe follows)
Vegetable Hash (page 146)
2 (1- to 1½-pound) pork
  tenderloins
Vegetable oil as needed
1 tablespoon Creole Meat
  Seasoning (page 156)

Light grill to get coals hot. Prepare Spicy Fig Sauce; reserve, keeping warm. Prepare Vegetable Hash through cutting of asparagus; reserve.

Remove all the tough silverskin from tenderloins. Rub tenderloins with oil and meat seasoning. Turning every couple of minutes, grill tenderloins over hot coals about 15 minutes. Check internal temperature with a digital stem meat thermometer. When temperature reaches 150 to 160 degrees, remove from grill and let rest 5 minutes or more for meat juices to set.

Complete preparation of Vegetable Hash. Cut each tender into 6 to 9 slices, depending on size of tenderloins. Serve on platter surrounded with Vegetable Hash and top meat with reserved Spicy Fig Sauce.

Chef's Tips: Pork tenderloins are readily available at the grocery. We used to cook pork very well done (but tough); now, however, that's not the case. Since trichinae are killed at 137 degrees, experts recommend cooking pork to 150 and no more than 165 degrees, which yields a medium- to just well-done, tender product.

Also may be roasted in 375-degree oven to desired doneness.

## SPICY FIG SAUCE

Yield: 1½ cups

*Chef's Note: The richness of the Demi-Glacé and figs in tandem with a wisp of praline flavor and the heat of jalapeño forms a hot/fruit/sweet sauce suited to a host of different meats.*

1 cup Veal or Beef Demi-Glacé
  (page 157)
1 teaspoon unsalted butter
2 tablespoons thinly sliced shallots
8 figs, quartered
½ jalapeño pepper, thinly sliced,
  divided
3 tablespoons praline liqueur
Salt and black pepper to taste
Touch of whipping cream

Prepare Veal or Beef Demi-Glacé; reserve until needed.

Heat butter in a small saucepan over medium heat; add shallots and sauté until translucent. Add figs and half the jalapeño; sauté until figs are warm. Add liqueur and reduce liquid by half; add reserved Demi-Glacé and simmer 2 to 3 minutes, or until sauce is hot.

Adjust seasoning with salt and pepper. A touch of cream will lighten the sauce if it's too spicy. If you want more pizazz, add remaining jalapeño.

Chef's Tips: Fresh figs are always best but dried figs are an acceptable choice as well. If using dried, place figs in a 1-cup measuring cup with 2 tablespoons water and microwave on high 30 to 60 seconds to soften. Let stand 5 minutes and pour off any liquid before adding to the recipe. The praline liqueur injects a touch of sweetness and nutty flavor that brings this sauce together. Some fresh jalapeños are hotter than others, so err on the cautious side to avoid a painful surprise for the uninitiated.

## Oatmeal-Crusted Pork Loin

Yield: 6 servings

*Chef's Note: This dish took second place in a cook-off sponsored by the National Pork Producers Council. To be honest, this was one of those times when I came up with a crazy last-minute idea and entered it in the contest. The opportunity to be creative every day is one of the things that makes cooking so much fun and such a challenge.*

1 recipe Crawfish and Andouille
  Stuffing (page 141)
1 recipe Jack Daniel's Molasses
  Vinegar (page 151)
6 (5-ounce) boneless pork loin
  cutlets, butterflied
3 teaspoons Creole Meat
  Seasoning, (page 156) divided
1½ cups uncooked quick oats
½ cup all-purpose flour
1½ tablespoons brown sugar
1½ tablespoons minced
  fresh parsley
2 tablespoons unsalted butter,
  melted
3 tablespoons orange juice
Vegetable oil as needed
6 (⅛-inch thick) slices onion

Prepare Crawfish and Andouille Stuffing; reserve until needed. Prepare Jack Daniel's Molasses Vinegar; reserve until needed. Preheat oven to 350 degrees.
  Lay cutlets on flat surface; pound to ¼-inch thickness. See Chef's Tip. Lightly season each cutlet with Creole Meat Seasoning, using about 2 teaspoons. Place ½ cup reserved stuffing on each cutlet; roll it up and secure with a toothpick.

Important: only lightly mix oats, flour, sugar, parsley, 1 teaspoon Creole Meat Seasoning, butter and orange juice in a large bowl. Coat each pork roll completely in oatmeal mixture by pressing mixture onto roll with your hands to get a nice even coating.
  Heat ½ cup oil in a large ovenproof skillet over medium-high heat; brown pork rolls on all sides. You may need to brown half, clean out oatmeal crumbs from skillet and repeat until all are browned. Remove from skillet and place onion slices in bottom of skillet. Place pork rolls back on top of onion slices. Roast in oven until pork reaches an internal temperature of 165 degrees, about 20 minutes.
  When pork is done, remove from oven and let rest about 10 minutes. Slice rolls into 1½-inch medallions. Place onion slices on a serving platter and arrange medallions on top. Drizzle with reserved warm Jack Daniel's Molasses Vinegar.

Chef's Tips: Buy lean pork cutlets, about 5 ounces each. To butterfly, use a knife to slice cutlet horizontally almost in half. Be careful not to cut all the way through. Lay cutlet open on a sheet of plastic wrap and cover with another sheet of plastic wrap. Use a meat mallet to lightly pount cutlets to about ¼-inch thickness.

Accompany this wonderful dish with one of the Sweet Potato Mashers (page 138-139).

Or, substitute boneless, skinless whole chicken breasts, pounded to ¼-inch thickness and your choice of stuffing.

Our Creole Oyster Stuffing (page 143) is a winning option for the crawfish stuffing in this recipe.

*"Never apologize for, or be ashamed of, your own taste in wine. Preferences for wines vary just as much as those for art or music."*
*— Humbrecht Duijker*

Oatmeal-Crusted Pork Loin

## SHRIMP-STUFFED CHICKEN BREAST

Yield: 6 servings

*Chef's Note: Imagine all things cheesy and good plumping up a chicken breast. Then, after baking, the chicken is sliced and fanned on the diagonal so that the delectable, multicolored stuffing is showcased. You'll be tempted to set speed records to eat this wonderful entrée. It certainly wins the popularity contest for luncheons and festive events.*

1 recipe Shrimp Stuffing
   (recipe follows)
6 (8-ounce) whole boneless,
   skinless chicken breasts
1 1/2 tablespoons Creole
   Meat Seasoning (page 156)
1 recipe Sun-Dried Tomato and
   Basil Beurre Blanc (page 155)

Prepare Shrimp Stuffing; reserve refrigerated until needed. Preheat oven to 375 degrees.

Place chicken between 2 layers of plastic wrap and pound slightly to 1/4-inch thickness. Season both sides of chicken with Creole Meat Seasoning. Place 1/2 cup reserved stuffing in center of each breast. Roll breast around stuffing; secure with a toothpick. Place chicken rolls, seam side down, on a lightly oiled baking sheet. Bake until chicken reaches an internal temperature of 165 degrees, about 30 to 35 minutes. Meanwhile, prepare Sun-Dried Tomato and Basil Beurre Blanc; reserve, keeping warm.

Let chicken rest 5 minutes, remove toothpicks and slice each breast on the bias into thirds. Fan chicken breast on individual plates or a meat platter; top with reserved Sun-Dried Tomato and Basil Beurre Blanc.

Chef's Tip: If you are allergic to shellfish, opt for sliced mushrooms in place of the shrimp. Accompany this entrée with Popcorn Rice (page 140).

## SHRIMP STUFFING

Yield: 3 cups

2 tablespoons vegetable oil
1/3 cup finely chopped
   red bell pepper
1/3 cup finely chopped green
   bell pepper
1/3 cup finely chopped red onion
1/2 pound (90/110 count) shrimp,
   peeled and deveined
1/2 tablespoon Creole
   Seafood Seasoning
1 tablespoon Louisiana
   hot pepper sauce
1 tablespoon Worcestershire sauce
1/2 cup water
1 (10-ounce) package fresh spinach,
   stemmed and washed
1 (3-ounce) package cream cheese,
   softened
2 ounces soft goat cheese
2 ounces feta cheese
Salt and black pepper to taste
Tabasco sauce

Heat oil in a large skillet over medium-high heat. Add red and green bell peppers, onion and shrimp; sauté until vegetables are tender. Spread out in a colander to drain excess liquid. Season with Creole Seafood Seasoning, hot sauce and Worcestershire; chill in refrigerator.

Place water in a large skillet over medium-high heat. When simmering, add spinach and cook until just wilted. Drain in colander and run under cold water to stop the cooking process. Use your hands to squeeze out as much water as possible; it's important to get spinach as dry as possible. Coarsely chop and refrigerate until needed.

When shrimp mixture is chilled, combine in a large bowl with spinach, cream cheese, goat cheese and feta. Season with salt, pepper and Tabasco. Reserve stuffing in refrigerator until needed. May be made day in advance.

*"An empty stomach is not a good political advisor."*
*— Albert Einstein*

Shrimp-Stuffed Chicken Breast

## SPICED PUMPKIN SEED CHICKEN

Yield: 4 servings

*Chef's Note: It was pure serendipity when Creole Chef Jose Arevalo created this dish. He eyed pumpkin seeds in the pantry, envisioned a spring vegetable hash to accompany the entrée, and came up with the final touch of a Sazerac Demi-Glacé. We salute the result!*

1 cup Sazerac Demi-Glacé
  (page 103)
2 cups pumpkin seeds
2½ tablespoons Creole Meat
  Seasoning, (page 156) divided
2 tablespoons Louisiana
  hot pepper sauce
2 tablespoons Worcestershire sauce
½ cup dry bread crumbs
Vegetable Hash (page 146)
4 (8-ounce) boneless, skinless
  whole chicken breasts
½ cup all-purpose flour
1 egg
1 cup milk
½ to 1 cup vegetable oil

Prepare Sazerac Demi-Glacé; reserve. Preheat oven to 250 degrees. Mix pumpkin seeds, 1 tablespoon Creole Meat Seasoning, hot sauce and Worcestershire in medium bowl. Spread pumpkin seed mixture on a baking sheet; roast until dry and crispy, about 10 to 20 minutes.

Preheat oven to 350 degrees. Cool seed mixture to room temperature. Then pulse in food processor until all seeds are coarsely chopped. Combine seed mixture with bread crumbs in a medium bowl; set aside. Prepare Vegetable Hash through cutting asparagus; reserve.

102

Spiced Pumpkin Seed Chicken

Season chicken with 1 table-spoon Creole Meat Seasoning. In a small bowl, combine flour with remaining ½ tablespoon Meat Seasoning; dust chicken with seasoned flour. In another bowl, combine egg and milk; dip chicken into egg wash. Coat chicken with reserved pumpkin seed mixture.

Bring ½ cup oil almost to smoking point in a large skillet over medium-high heat. Sear half of chicken in hot oil on each side. If oil starts to burn, use remaining ½ cup oil to sear remaining chicken. Arrange chicken on a baking sheet. Place in oven until internal temperature of chicken reaches 165 degrees, about 15 minutes.

Complete Vegetable Hash recipe; reserve, keeping warm. To serve, place Vegetable Hash on serving platter and top with chicken; finish with a drizzle of reserved Sazerac Demi-Glacé.

**Chef's Tip:** To ensure chicken remains moist while baking, thinly slice some onion, scatter on the baking sheet and place chicken breasts on top.

## SAZERAC DEMI-GLACÉ

Yield: 1 cup

*Chef's Note: The renowned New Orleans Sazerac Cocktail inspired this magically potent sauce, which will light up other meats like pork tenderloin or venison that may be tucked away in the freezer.*

½ cup Beef or Veal Demi-Glacé (page 69)
¼ cup sugar
¼ cup water, boiling
1 teaspoon vegetable oil
1 tablespoon finely chopped shallots
3 tablespoons Jack Daniel's Whiskey
2 teaspoons Angostura bitters
Salt to taste

Prepare Beef or Veal Demi-Glacé; reserve, keeping warm until needed. Combine sugar and water in a 1-cup measure. Stir until sugar is dissolved; set aside. Heat oil in a small saucepan over medium-high heat; add shallots and sauté until translu-cent. Add whiskey, bitters and reserved sugar/water mixture. Cook over medium heat to reduce sauce until just syrupy; don't let sugar caramelize. Add reserved demi-glacé and season with salt. Serve warm.

## GRILLED CHICKEN IN ANDOUILLE MUSTARD SAUCE

Yield: 6 servings

*Chef's Note: Your family will never guess how completely care-free it is to produce this dish. The spicy andouille sausage and Creole mustard create their own special party for your palate.*

6 (8-ounce) boneless, skinless chicken breasts
Vegetable oil as needed
1 tablespoon Creole Meat Seasoning (page 156)
1 cup (¼-inch slices, cut in half) andouille or spicy smoked sausage
1 cup quartered button mushrooms
1½ cups whipping cream
½ cup Creole mustard
Salt and black pepper to taste
2 tablespoons thinly sliced green onion

If grilling, heat coals. If roasting in oven, preheat oven to 350 degrees. Rub chicken with oil and season with Creole Meat Seasoning; set aside. Grill chick-en over hot coals to an internal temperature of 165 degrees. Or, roast in oven about 20 to 25 minutes.

In a large hot skillet, cook sausage over medium-high heat until fat is rendered. Add mush-rooms and sauté 1 minute. Stir in cream. Reduce temperature and simmer to reduce liquid by one-fourth original volume; add mustard. Simmer to reduce sauce until it coats the back of a spoon. Season with salt and pep-per. Arrange grilled/roasted chicken on a meat platter and top with andouille sausage; gar-nish with onion.

**Chef's Tip:** Grill or roast a whole, cut-up chicken rather than just skinless breasts. Two favorite accompaniments to this luscious entrée are Maple-Glazed Carrots with Rosemary (page 140) and Popcorn Rice (page 140).

104

Sous Chef Randy Evans works on the line.

*"The so-called nouvelle cuisine usually means not enough on your plate and too much on your bill."*
— *Paul Bocuse*

## CHICKEN PONTALBA

Yield: 6 servings

*Chef's Note: This distinctive classic was created by Paul Blangé, one of the Brennan family's first great chefs and named after Baroness Pontalba, who came to New Orleans in the 1700s. We put a different spin on it by coating the chicken with crispy shredded potatoes.*

1 cup vegetable oil, divided
1½ cups thinly sliced button
    mushrooms
1½ cups medium diced Canadian
    bacon (about 9 ounces)
⅓ cup thinly sliced green onion
6 cups shoestring potatoes
½ cup softened goat cheese
½ cup crumbled feta cheese
Salt and black pepper to taste
6 (6-ounce) whole boneless,
    skinless chicken breasts
4 tablespoons Creole Meat
    Seasoning, (page 155) divided
2 cups all-purpose flour
3 eggs
2 cups milk
1 recipe Tomato Tarragon Beurre
    Blanc (page 155)

Heat 2 tablespoons oil in a large skillet over medium-high heat. Add mushrooms and bacon; sauté 2 to 3 minutes, or until mushrooms are soft. Stir in onion; remove from heat. Cover and chill in refrigerator at least 1 hour.

Prepare shoestring potatoes; place in bowl of cold water to prevent discoloration; reserve. Once mushroom mixture is chilled, fold in goat cheese and feta; season with salt and pepper. Reserve stuffing, keeping cold until ready to use.

Preheat oven to 400 degrees. Place chicken breasts between two sheets of plastic wrap and pound to ¼-inch thickness. Season both sides of each breast with ½ teaspoon Creole Meat Seasoning; place ½ cup reserved stuffing mixture in center of each breast. Roll breast around stuffing and secure with a toothpick. Dust chicken in flour. Combine eggs and milk in a small bowl; dip chicken into egg wash and dredge in flour; set aside.

When ready to use potatoes, drain well and pat dry on paper towels. In a medium bowl, combine potatoes with remaining 2 tablespoons Creole Meat Seasoning. Carefully remove toothpick and press seasoned potatoes around chicken rolls.

In a large nonstick skillet, bring remaining oil to smoking point, then reduce heat to medium. Oil should be ¼ inch deep in skillet. Sear chicken until potatoes are golden brown, about 1 to 2 minutes per side. Place chicken on baking sheet lightly sprayed with nonstick vegetable spray; bake until chicken reaches an internal temperature of 165 degrees, about 25 to 30 minutes.

Prepare Tomato Tarragon Beurre Blanc; reserve, keeping warm. To serve, spoon a scant ¼ cup Beurre Blanc sauce on each plate. Cut chicken breast in half and place over sauce.

Chef's Tips: A handy tool for your kitchen is a mandoline. There are now economical versions for the home kitchen made with a plastic frame and a variety of attachments. The blade we use is the one for shoestring potatoes. Be extremely careful not to cut more than the potato. The device doesn't distinguish fingers from potatoes very well!

When preparing this dish, you might prefer to only use a skillet and eliminate the additional oven baking. If so, add more oil to the skillet for a golden crust while cooking the chicken to an internal temperature of 165 degrees.

Centerpiece with flowers and vegetables

## HUNTING AND COOKING

I love being outdoors at the hunting lease I share with several chefs. Some think we're really there just to eat. We roast wild pig on the spit or skewer ducks marinated in Grand Marnier over an open fire or roast a fresh venison ham. At night we enjoy the stars, cigars and wonder what the people at the restaurant are doing. We regularly serve game at the restaurant. I use my professional knowledge of game to improve my personal cooking style — like cutting venison into restaurant-style cuts. For example, I have venison chops or medallions from the backstrap. One Christmas I took the rib racks and made an awesome crown roast, with a mountain of cornbread dressing in the center.

Guests at chef's table in the kitchen

### TEXAS BOBWHITE QUAIL

Yield: 4 servings

*Chef's Note: Bobwhite quail is a very popular game bird in Texas, as well as Missouri, where I grew up. This recipe is a world away from the fried quail and cream gravy my granny used to fix.*

4 cups Creole Oyster Stuffing (page 143)
1 recipe Candied-Pecan Sweet Potatoes (page 139)
8 Bobwhite quail, semi-boneless
4 teaspoons Creole Meat Seasoning (page 156)
Vegetable oil as needed
8 (1/8-inch thick) slices yellow onion
1 cup Homemade Worcestershire Glaze (page 154)

Prepare Creole Oyster Stuffing; reserve until needed. Prepare Candied-Pecan Sweet Potatoes; reserve, keeping warm. Preheat oven to 375 degrees.

Rinse quail under cold running water, inside and out. Season quail with Creole Meat Seasoning. Divide reserved stuffing into 8 equal portions, about 1/2 cup each, and stuff cavities of quail. "Round" the quail to give some shape; then cross the legs and stick a toothpick through both legs into the quail. Rub each quail with oil and set onto an onion slice placed in bottom of an ovenproof roasting pan large enough to hold all 8 quail. Roast quail 25 minutes. Check quail in center of stuffing with a digital stem meat thermometer to ensure that internal temperature is 165 degrees.

While quail are roasting, prepare Homemade Worcestershire Glaze; reserve, keeping warm. Remove quail from oven and keep warm until ready to serve. Remove toothpicks. Arrange quail, each on its onion nest, on a large platter. Place a heaping mound of reserved Candied-Pecan Sweet Potatoes in center of platter. Drizzle reserved Worcestershire Glaze over quail.

Chef Tips: Throughout the country, there are game bird farms to buy freshly dressed birds. These are the best. However, frozen quail are available in a lot of flagship grocery stores and are usually semi-boneless. Or check the Source Guide (page 186) for semi-boneless Bobwhite quail. The best is get someone else to bone them, and you cook them.

If that's not possible, to bone a quail you'll need a pair of kitchen shears and a small sharp knife. First, clip off wings at the joint. Next, break the back and pull out part of the backbone. Turn the quail inside out, pulling out the rest of the backbone. To remove breastbone, look for any little rib bones or wish bone that can be pulled out. Leave in leg bones, breaking them loose from the pelvic bone. After you've done a few hundred of these, you will have it down pat!

Substitute Crawfish and Andouille Stuffing (page 141) for Oyster Stuffing in this recipe.

Texas Bobwhite Quail

## RINGNECK PHEASANT AND FOIE GRAS

Yield: 4 servings

*Chef's Note: Just say "pheasant," and you'll transport me right back to the Iowa cornfields — hunting with Dad. Even better than the hunt was when we'd fry or roast our day's take. I carry over those tremendous times by preparing pheasant any number of ways for our guests. Far from Iowa, in Texas we elegantly embellish this topnotch game bird with sweet-and-sour Braised Red Cabbage, unbeatable Yukon Gold fingerling potatoes and a duet of melt-in-your-mouth foie gras and tantalizing Fresh Berry Demi-Glacé.*

2 tablespoons butter
2 cups coarsely chopped onion
1 cup coarsely chopped carrot
1 cup coarsely chopped celery
2 (2¹/₂-pound) pheasants, cleaned
Vegetable oil as needed
2 tablespoons Creole Meat
   Seasoning (page 156)
Bacon as needed, about ¹/₂ pound
12 Yukon Gold potatoes, small
   fingerlings, washed, not peeled
Braised Red Cabbage (page 110)
Fresh Berry Demi-Glacé (page 110)
4 (2-ounce) slices Foie Gras
Salt and black pepper to taste

Preheat oven to 375 degrees. Heat butter in a medium skillet over medium-high heat; add onion, carrot and celery. Sauté just until softened, about 5 minutes; set mirepoix aside.

Rinse pheasants under cold running water. Coat pheasants with oil and dust with Creole Meat Seasoning. Stuff cavity with some of reserved mirepoix. Add remaining mirepoix to a large roasting pan and place pheasants on top of vegetables. Cover pheasant breasts with bacon; this will help retain moisture during roasting. Scatter potatoes in pan. Roast pheasant about 45 to 60 minutes. Remove from oven when internal temperature measures 145 degrees, before pheasant is completely cooked. When checking pheasant, prick potatoes to see if they are just tender. When they are, remove from pan and reserve. Cut potatoes in half lengthwise when cool.

While pheasant is roasting, prepare Braised Red Cabbage; reserve, keeping warm. Prepare Fresh Berry Demi-Glacé; reserve, keeping warm.

When pheasant is cool enough to handle, remove bacon and reserve. Starting at top of breast, cut along the breastbone, body cavity and at wing joint to remove a breast half. Repeat procedure to remove remaining 3 breast halves. Remove legs at the pelvic joint and leave whole. Save all bones, legs and pan drippings for future use.

Near serving time, place pheasant breast back on top of vegetables in roasting pan. Re-cover breast with reserved bacon and finish roasting, about 15 minutes. When done, remove bacon. Strain drippings into a small bowl; stir into reserved Fresh Berry Demi-Glacé.

Meanwhile, sear foie gras in a medium skillet about 1 minute on each side; remove and keep warm. In same pan, add potatoes and sauté in foie gras fat; season with salt and pepper.

To serve, place about 1 cup reserved Braised Red Cabbage in center of each plate and arrange a pheasant breast half on top. Surround cabbage with 6 potato halves and top pheasant with foie gras. Drizzle remaining foie gras fat over potatoes; drizzle pheasant with reserved Fresh Berry Demi-Glacé. Serve immediately.

Chef's Tip: Pheasant is a very lean, white-meated bird, so be careful not to over cook. The trio of sautéed onion, carrot and celery forms what chefs call a "mirepoix" (mihr-PWAH). For this dish, mirepoix functions to season the pheasant as a stuffing and to supply an aromatic bed for the bird to rest on during roasting.

109

Ringneck Pheasant and Foie Gras

*Brennan's*

*Life is short... eat well!*

## CUSTOMER – EYEZING

In designing our new kitchen, Alex found the original 1967 plans showing 12 can openers. Today, our guests demand the best, freshest products available, thus refrigeration and cutting boards are more important than can storage or openers. To be sure, those demands are noted daily. In fact, our management training stresses developing "customer eyes." Doing the same things day-in and day-out, as manager, hostess or waiter, we may overlook things that customers pick out quickly. Thus, every day we sit at every table, walk from front to back — as a customer might — to see what they might see. We don't just maintain the status quo — continual improvement sometimes comes in the smallest packages.

## BRAISED RED CABBAGE

4 bacon strips, cut into
  1/4-inch pieces
1 1/2 teaspoons brown sugar
4 cups shredded red cabbage
4 cups shredded savoy cabbage
1 tablespoon red wine
1 tablespoon rice wine vinegar
1 teaspoon caraway seeds
Salt and black pepper to taste

Sauté bacon in a large skillet over medium-high heat until crisp.
   Add sugar and stir to melt.
   Stir in red and savoy cabbages; sauté 3 to 4 minutes, or until cabbage starts to wilt.
   Add wine, vinegar and caraway seeds; cook about 5 minutes, or until cabbage is tender.
   Season with salt and pepper; reserve, keeping warm until serving.

## FRESH BERRY DEMI-GLACÉ

1 cup Veal Demi-Glacé (page 69)
1 tablespoon unsalted butter
1 shallot, minced
1/2 cup brandy
1 cup fresh blueberries
  or raspberries
2 tablespoons whipping cream
Salt and black pepper to taste

Prepare Veal Demi-Glacé; reserve until needed.
   Heat butter in a small saucepan over medium heat; add shallots and sauté until translucent.
   Add brandy: Take care to avoid a possible flame up when adding brandy. Stir in berries and reserved Veal Demi-Glacé; bring to a low simmer. Stir in cream.
   Season with salt and pepper; keep warm.

## CAMOUFLAGE CARL'S ROASTED DUCK

Yield: 1–2 servings

Allow one small or one-half large duck per person

*Chef's Note: The only ducks I hunt are those that I eat. My favorites are teal, pintail or mallard, but I'll never turn down a good duck when offered. When it comes to geese, I prefer White-fronted (Specklebelly) and Canada.*

For each duck:
1 tablespoon olive oil
1 tablespoon butter

Marinade:
1 large dressed duck
2 cups red wine
1 cup Grand Marnier
1 cup orange marmalade
2 medium oranges, quartered
8 to 12 sprigs of fresh oregano
2 cups coarsely chopped onions
2 cups coarsely chopped celery
1/2 teaspoon salt
1 teaspoon freshly ground black
  pepper
1 teaspoon olive oil
2 cups chicken broth
Salt and black pepper to taste
Sprigs of fresh herbs to garnish

   Rinse duck with cold water. Remove giblets and excess fat. Set aside. In a large stainless or glass bowl mix wine, Grand Marnier, marmalade, oranges, oregano, onions, celery, salt and pepper. Take 2 cups of the marinade mixture and stuff the cavilty of the duck. Marinate the duck in remaining marinade for at least 2 hours or overnight.

If marinating overnight, cover bowl with plastic wrap and refrigerate. Remove bird and reserve marinade.

When ready to cook, preheat oven to 325 degrees.

Add olive oil to Dutch oven or roasting pan and lightly brown bird on all sides. Remove bird to a side dish. Pour the marinade, including the fruit, onions and celery, into the bottom of the Dutch oven or roasting pan. Add broth. Place the whole bird on top; cover pan. Roast 1½ to 2 hours, until tender, occasionally basting with pan juices.

Remove the duck from the cooking pan; carve breast meat and legs from carcass, keeping breast halves intact. Reserve, keeping warm until needed.

Skim fat and reduce the pot drippings over medium-high heat to about ½ cup; strain. Season sauce to taste with salt and pepper.

To serve slice breast into ¼-inch diagonal pieces; fan out on serving plate. Add one leg per serving. Drizzle with warm sauce. Decorate with herb sprigs.

Chef's Tip: For extra heat I add a thinly sliced jalapeño. Feel free to substitute other fruits or wines Serve with Texas Cornbread Pudding (page 143) or Warm Potato Salad (page 144).

Thomas Franklin, distinguished in Brennan's of Houston hospitality for over three decades.

## PORTOBELLO MUSHROOM NAPOLEON

Yield: 2 entrée servings or 4 appetizer or side dishes

*Chef's Note: Although one usually thinks of a napoleon as a dessert, this is a savory rendition well worth the steps of preparation. We call portobellos "Vegetarian Steak."*

1 (14.5-ounce) can Cajun or
　　Creole stewed tomatoes
Salt and black pepper to taste
Nonstick cooking spray as needed
1 red bell pepper, roasted
　　and julienned
1 green bell pepper, roasted
　　and julienned
1 yellow bell pepper, roasted
　　and julienned
3 large Portobello mushrooms,
　　stems removed
1 tablespoon Creole Seafood
　　Seasoning (page 157)
2/3 cup Creamed Spinach (page 75)
1 teaspoon minced garlic
1 teaspoon finely chopped
　　fresh basil
1 teaspoon finely chopped
　　fresh thyme
1 teaspoon finely chopped
　　fresh oregano
1/2 cup all-purpose flour
1 teaspoon Creole Seafood
　　Seasoning (page 157)
1 egg, slightly beaten
2 tablespoons milk
1/4 cup vegetable oil
Fresh thyme or rosemary for
　　garnish (optional)

Place tomatoes in a small saucepan and cook over low heat about 15 minutes, or until a sauce-like consistency. Season with salt and pepper. May be made ahead and refrigerated. Warm before using.

Spray red, green and yellow bell peppers with nonstick cooking spray and roast using Chef's Tip following; reserve. Coat mushroom caps with nonstick cooking spray and sprinkle with 1 tablespoon Creole Seafood Seasoning. Place mushrooms on a sheet pan; broil 2 to 3 minutes on each side. Remove from broiler and cool in refrigerator on sheet pan.

Prepare Creamed Spinach; reserve, keeping warm. Place reserved peppers in a small bowl with garlic, basil, thyme, oregano, salt and pepper; reserve. Preheat oven to 375 degrees.

Slice mushroom caps horizontally in half to yield 6 disc shapes. Reserve 2 of the nicest tops; set aside for later use.

To create Napoleon: Place the 2 largest portobello slices on a lightly greased sheet pan, place 1/3 cup reserved Creamed Spinach on each slice, top with another mushroom slice, and then top each with half the reserved pepper mixture. When ready to serve, bake about 15 minutes, or until hot throughout.

Combine flour and 1 teaspoon Creole Seafood Seasoning in a small bowl. In another small bowl, mix egg and milk. Heat oil in a medium skillet over medium-high heat. Dust the 2 reserved mushroom caps in seasoned flour, dip into egg wash and dredge back into flour mixture. Sauté mushroom caps in

hot skillet about 1 to 1½ minutes each side, or until golden brown on both sides.

To serve, pour half the reserved tomato sauce onto each plate and top with hot Napoleon straight out of the oven. Cut sautéed tops in half and arrange criss-cross over each Napoleon. Spear with a sprig of thyme or rosemary to hold in place and decorate.

**Chef's Tips: To roast a bell pepper, rub pepper with oil or spray with nonstick cooking spray and place on a baking sheet. Broil pepper until it is well blistered on all sides, about 10 minutes. Remove pepper from broiler and place in a bowl. Cover bowl with plastic wrap and allow pepper to steam about 15 minutes. When pepper is cool, scrape off charred skin with a small knife. Cut pepper in half length-wise, remove seeds and wipe clean; cut into julienne strips.**

**Also, substitute or add other vegetables such as very thinly sliced and lightly grilled zucchini or yellow squash.**

**At the restaurant, we use the Creole sauce base from our Louisiana Shrimp Creole (page 128) for this recipe.**

Portobello Mushroom Napoleon

brennan's favorites

Living near the Gulf of Mexico creates many opportunities to use fresh fish, and we capitalize on that freshness in the Creole tradition. Always open to suggestions, I took a tip from Dick Brennan, Sr. early in my career, grated some potatoes and developed Potato-Crusted Fish Lyonnaise — another favorite at Brennan's of Houston and our New Orleans restaurants. Being so near the coast, oysters in any fashion also reign as favorites.

A most-requested dish is our Pecan Fish — we present the best fish available each day. We use Texas pecans, roast them, grind them up and then coat the fish in the delectable pecan crust and present it with more pecan pieces sprinkled on top. It's excellent with Popcorn Rice.

To be sure, you'll find the Creole-Cajun mainstay, crawfish, in our appetizers, salads, brunch dishes and main dishes. Our guests impatiently await crawfish season each year. We buy sacks of live crawfish to fill the demand for Crawfish Kacal, Crawfish Etouffée, Fried Crawfish Salad — you get the picture. At home, my friends love my all-in-one-pot crawfish boils. Spicy crawfish paired with a favorite, icy adult beverage is a party waiting to happen.

We pride ourselves on transforming the ordinary to extraordinary, so head for the kitchen and get cooking!

Potato-Crusted Fish Lyonnaise

Southern Pecan Fish

Spiced Pecans (page 25)
Creole Meunière Sauce (page 150)
1½ cups dried bread crumbs
4 (6-ounce) Gulf fish fillets
1 tablespoon Creole Seafood
   Seasoning, (page 157) divided
½ cup all-purpose flour
1 egg
½ cup milk
½ cup vegetable oil

Prepare Spiced Pecans; reserve. Prepare Creole Meuniere Sauce; reserve, keeping warm. Heat oven to 350 degrees.

Pulse Spiced Pecans in food processor until mixture is fine, but not oily. Blend in bread crumbs; set aside until needed. Lightly season fillets with 2 teaspoons Creole Seafood Seasoning. In a small bowl, combine flour with remaining 1 teaspoon Creole Seafood Seasoning; dust fillets with seasoned flour.

In another small bowl, combine egg and milk; dip fillets into egg wash. Coat fillets with reserved pecan mixture.

Heat oil almost to smoking point in a large skillet. Sauté fillets until they are a "seared" brown color on each side. Place on a baking sheet and finish in oven, about 10 minutes or until done.

Serve with reserved Creole Meunière Sauce. Accompany with Popcorn Rice (page 140) and a sauté of green vegetables.

## SOUTHERN PECAN FISH

Yield: 4 servings

*Chef's Note: The No. 1 signature fish dish on our menu has had an intriguing metamorphosis. Historically, this entrée was made with trout in the days when speckled sea trout was abundant. We sautéed a fillet and topped it with a handful of Southern pecans. Since we are always trying to elevate classics to new heights, we now coat the entire fillet with spiced, roasted pecans and lace it with a rich Creole Meunière Sauce.*

Chef's Tip: Use the Spiced Pecan crust on chicken cooked the same way.

116

## CHICKEN-FRIED CATFISH

Yield: 4 servings

*Chef's Note: One of the premier Texas state dishes is chicken-fried steak. Our twist is to chicken-fry small fillets of fish! Team them with Warm Potato Salad (page 144) and you'll vow life was never better.*

1 cup Ravigote Sauce (page 49)
Warm Potato Salad
   (see recipe, page 144)
Vegetable oil for deep frying
8 (3-ounce) catfish fillets
1½ tablespoons Creole Seafood
   Seasoning, (page 157) divided
1 egg
½ cup milk
1 cup corn meal
1 cup all-purpose flour
2 finely-diced shallots

Prepare Ravigote Sauce; reserve until needed. Prepare Warm Potato Salad; reserve, keeping warm, until needed. Heat oil in deep fryer to 325 to 350 degrees.

Season fillets with ½ tablespoon Creole Seafood Seasoning; set aside. In a small bowl, combine egg and milk. In another medium bowl, combine cornmeal, flour, shallots and remaining 1 tablespoon Creole Seafood Seasoning.

Dip fillets into egg wash and then dredge in cornmeal mixture. Deep fry fillets 2 to 3 minutes, or until fillets float to the surface. Drain fillets on paper towels.

To serve, cross 2 fillets on top of reserved Warm Potato Salad, then drizzle reserved Ravigote Sauce over top.

Chef's Tips: Again I recommend using a deep skillet method to cook this fish. Use enough oil to come halfway up, or a little more, on the fish. DO NOT HEAT OIL OVER 375 DEGREES. For this recipe, it's best to fry fish at 325 to 350 degrees.

I like to drizzle some Remoulade Sauce (page 31) over the fried fish. Garnish with something as simple as a little bunch of alfalfa sprouts, tossed in vinaigrette, placed on top of fish.

## FLOUNDER VERONIQUE

Yield: 4 servings

*Chef's Note: "Veronique" is the title given to a sublime dish that uses seedless white grapes. Our talented former sous chef, Mark Holley, worked his Creole magic with this version.*

1 cup Champagne Fennel Cream
   (page 150)
4 (6-ounce) flounder fillets
Vegetable oil as needed
Salt and black pepper to taste
½ pound jumbo lump crabmeat,
   cleaned and picked over
½ cup seedless green grapes,
   unpeeled and cut in half
   lengthwise
Juice of ½ lime

Prepare Champagne Fennel Cream; reserve, keeping warm. Preheat oven to 400 degrees.

Rub fillets with a small amount of oil; season with salt and pepper. Place fillets skin side down on a baking sheet sprayed with nonstick cooking spray

and roast in oven until cooked through, about 8 to 10 minutes. Heat 1 tablespoon oil in a large skillet over medium-high heat and quickly sauté crabmeat. Add reserved Champagne Fennel Cream, grapes and lime juice; season with salt and pepper.

Serve fillets topped with Champagne Fennel Cream sauce.

Chef Tips: When in season and available, champagne grapes are spectacular for this recipe. There is no need to cut champagne grapes in half due to their miniature size. If the Champagne Fennel Cream Sauce is a touch thick, thin it with another splash of champagne. A squeeze of lime or lemon juice definitely pops out the flavor of cream sauces like this.

Substitute salmon, snapper or another mild, flaky fish in this recipe. I like to place a sprig of fennel on top of each fillet as a finishing touch.

I recommend presenting this dish with sides of blanched jumbo asparagus and Popcorn Rice (page 140).

## GRILLED YELLOWFIN TUNA WITH CRABMEAT MANGO-PAPAYA RELISH

Yield: 6 servings

*Chef's Note: There are no two ways about it — this is simply a stellar recipe! It's carefree, light, sunny and will please any appetite.*

Crabmeat Mango-Papaya Relish
   (recipe follows)
6 (6- to 7-ounce) yellowfin tuna steaks
Vegetable oil as needed
1 1/2 tablespoons Creole Seafood
   Seasoning (page 157)

Prepare Crabmeat Mango-Papaya Relish; reserve.

Rub tuna with oil and sprinkle both sides of steaks with Creole Seafood Seasoning.

Grill fish over hot coals or roast in an oiled skillet over medium-high heat until desired doneness.

Top each tuna steak with 1/2 cup reserved Crabmeat Mango-Papaya Relish.

Chef's Tips: Optional choices for the tuna include salmon fillets, sword-fish steak or another grilled fish.

Feel free to substitute another fruit, such as assorted ripe melons, for mango and papaya.

## CRABMEAT MANGO-PAPAYA RELISH

Yield: 3 cups

1 cup chopped mango
1 cup chopped papaya
1 tablespoon finely chopped red
   bell pepper
2 tablespoons finely chopped
   red onion
1 tablespoon finely chopped
   poblano pepper
1 tablespoon rice wine vinegar
1 1/2 teaspoons honey
1/2 teaspoon finely chopped fresh basil
1/2 teaspoon finely chopped
   fresh oregano
1/2 pound jumbo lump crabmeat,
   cleaned and picked over
Salt and black pepper to taste

In a medium bowl, combine mango, papaya, red pepper, onion, poblano pepper, vinegar, honey, basil and oregano; mix well.

Gently fold in crabmeat; season with salt and pepper. Cover and refrigerate until needed.

Chef's Tip: Leave out the crabmeat to make a relish free of seafood.

Grilled Yellowfin Tuna with Crabmeat Mango-Papaya Relish

Gulf Fish Court Bouillon

## GULF FISH COURT BOUILLON

Yield: 2 servings

*Chef's Note: In Creole kitchens we pronounce this dish as one word, "koo-bee-yahn." It's a time-honored dish that we re-discovered by lightening it with fresh, fresh ingredients, eliminating the roux and presenting it "papillote" style. Instead of the traditional papillote parchment paper bag, I opted for heavy foil. We demonstrated this impressive entrée in Chicago at the National Restaurant Show in 1999 and 2000. We worked with Pat from the well-known Reynolds commercials!*

³/4 cup julienned fresh tomatoes (peeled and seeded before slicing)
¹/3 cup julienned onion
¹/2 cup julienned roasted peppers (red, green, and/or yellow)
2 garlic cloves, shaved thin
¹/3 cup thinly diagonally cut celery
¹/2 teaspoon Louisiana hot pepper sauce
¹/2 teaspoon Worcestershire sauce
2 tablespoons red wine
2 drops liquid crab boil
2 bay leaves
2 lemon wedges
¹/4 teaspoon salt
¹/4 teaspoon black pepper
2 (5-ounce) boneless, skinless red snapper fillets

6 large Gulf shrimp, peeled and deveined
3 tablespoons Creole Seafood Seasoning (page 157)

Preheat oven to 350 degrees. In a medium bowl, combine tomatoes, onion, peppers, garlic, celery, hot sauce, Worcestershire, wine, crab boil, bay leaves, lemon wedges, salt and pepper; set aside. Cut an 18x18-inch sheet of heavy-duty aluminum foil and lay flat on the counter. Season fillets and shrimp with Creole Seafood Seasoning. Place fillets, side by side, in center of foil and top each fillet with 3 shrimp. Place half of vegetable mixture on top of each fillet and shrimp.

Cut another 18x18-inch sheet of foil and cover fish; align it with bottom sheet. Fold edges of foil together tightly, folding over 3 to 4 times on each side. Then fold each corner a couple of times. (This helps lock in the heat.) Place foil bag on a baking sheet and bake 25 minutes. Foil will puff up when finished cooking. Carefully cut foil open (to avoid a steam burn) and spoon fish and vegetables onto a serving platter or into a bowl.

**Chef's Tips:** Feel free to use another fish — white, flaky fish works best. This is an easy throw-in-the-oven dish. You can substitute a melange of vegetables, add a touch of white wine and lemon, season and put it into the oven.

Use liquid crab boil sparingly! It is very intense and powerful.

## GULF SEAFOOD PONTCHARTRAIN

Yield: 6 servings

*Chef's Note: Words can't adequately describe what a magnificent dish this is. The Brennan's of Houston version of a Louisiana classic is a seafood lover's dream come true. If you're hungry for seafood, this is the dish I often recommend because of its variety of seafood.*

Pontchartrain Sauce
   (recipe follows)
6 (6-ounce) fillets (snapper,
   mahi mahi or trout)
Vegetable oil as needed

Creole Seafood Seasoning
   (page 157) as needed
1 pound (36/42 count) shrimp,
   peeled and deveined
18 raw oysters, shucked
1/2 pound jumbo lump crabmeat
1/2 cup Swiss chard, cut into strips
1/2 cup drained, canned
   diced tomatoes
Dash of Tabasco if needed

Prepare Pontchartrain Sauce; reserve, keeping warm. Preheat oven to 400 degrees.

Coat fillets with oil and season with 1 tablespoon Creole Seafood Seasoning. Place on a baking sheet and roast in oven until cooked through — cooking time will vary depending on what type of fish is used — usually about 10 minutes. Season shrimp with 1 tablespoon seafood seasoning. Heat 2 tablespoons oil in a large skillet over medium-high heat; sauté shrimp about 3 to 5 minutes.

Add reserved Pontchartrain Sauce to shrimp and lower heat to simmer. Add oysters, crabmeat, Swiss chard and tomatoes. Simmer until oysters start to curl and everything is hot; reserve, keeping warm. Adjust seasoning with Creole Seafood Seasoning and a dash of Tabasco if needed. Do not overstir — you don't want to break up the crabmeat.

To serve, place a fillet in center of each plate, top with reserved seafood Pontchartrain Sauce.

**Chef's Tip:** If you can't find one of the listed seafoods, use more of our seafood suggestions or your own favorites.

## PONTCHARTRAIN SAUCE

2 cups shrimp stock, fish stock or
   water
1 teaspoon Louisiana hot
   pepper sauce
1 teaspoon Worcestershire sauce
1/4 cup unsalted butter,
   room temperature
1/4 cup all-purpose flour
1 teaspoon Creole Seafood
   Seasoning (page 157)
2 tablespoons fresh lemon juice

In a medium saucepan, combine stock, hot sauce and Worcestershire; bring to a boil. In a small bowl, mix butter and flour until smooth; whisk into boiling liquid a piece at a time until sauce thickens to a slightly more than medium consistency.

Add Creole Seafood Seasoning, reduce to low heat and simmer 15 to 20 minutes. Remove from heat and stir in lemon juice; reserve, keeping warm until ready to use.

**Chef's Tip:** Look for frozen fish stock at the grocery.

*"Many excellent cooks are spoiled by going into the arts."*
*— Paul Gauguin*

## ALLISON INVITES HOUSTONIANS TO A SLEEP-OVER AND BREAKFAST AT BRENNAN'S

Breakfast at Brennan's of Houston took on new meaning on June 8, 2001. As we were wrapping up this cookbook, Tropical Storm Allison's fury drenched much of downtown and many outlying areas of our city. Late that Friday night the floodwaters swept away thousands of cars, preventing some diners and staff from leaving the restaurant. Ultimately, we provided white table cloths as bedding for about a dozen unexpected overnight guests. Our cooks braved the high water the next morning and prepared breakfast for all the stranded guests.

## POTATO-CRUSTED FISH LYONNAISE

Yield: 4 servings

*Chef's Note: One day Dick Brennan, Sr. was visiting from New Orleans. He sat me down and told me his vision for a fish dish. I headed straight to the kitchen, shredded some potatoes and figured out how to make them stick to a fish fillet. Just like the potatoes, Fish Lyonnaise has stuck around ever since. I like to dress this crusty entrée with a Lemon Beurre Blanc sauce, caramelized onions and a touch of fresh thyme.*

1 cup Lemon Beurre Blanc
  (page 155)
3 large potatoes
4 cups cold water
1 tablespoon minced
  fresh parsley
2 1/2 tablespoons Creole Seafood
  Seasoning, (page 157) divided
2 eggs
1/2 cup milk
1 cup all-purpose flour
4 (5-ounce) boneless, skinless red
  snapper fillets
1/2 cup plus 2 tablespoons
  vegetable oil, divided
1 cup julienned onion
1/2 teaspoon minced fresh thyme
Julienned tomato or caviar
  for garnish

Prepare Lemon Beurre Blanc; set aside and keep warm. Preheat oven to 350 degrees.

Peel potatoes, cut shoestring size on mandoline or shred on a grater (large-sized opening) and place in water. Squeeze potatoes dry. Put into a medium bowl and season with parsley and 1 tablespoon Creole Seafood Seasoning; set aside.

In a small bowl, combine eggs and milk. In another small bowl, season flour with 1 tablespoon Creole Seafood Seasoning. Season fillets with remaining 1/2 tablespoon Creole Seafood Seasoning, dredge in flour, dip into egg wash and again dredge in flour. Lightly press potatoes onto each side of fish fillets until fully crusted.

Heat 1/2 cup oil in a medium skillet over medium-high heat. Fry fillets 2 minutes on each side, or until golden brown. Transfer fish to sheet pan and finish in oven 5 to 7 minutes, or until done.

In a small skillet, heat remaining 2 tablespoons oil over medium-high heat. Add onion and sauté until golden brown.

To serve, add caramelized onion and thyme to reserved Lemon Beurre Blanc sauce. Ladle sauce onto each plate and top with fish; garnish fish with julienned tomato, caviar or another garnish of choice.

Chef's Tips: I recommend using a mandoline to shred the potatoes because it gives a nicer-looking crust. At home I use my dad's tried-and-true method. In a big, deep cast iron skillet fry the fish, adding enough oil to come at least halfway up the sides. DO NOT HEAT THE OIL TOO HOT — 325 to 350 degrees tops!

## SALMON AND SMOKED CORN SALSA

Yield: 4 servings

*Chef's Note: Attention salmon fans! If you look up "Southwest" in the dictionary, you're liable to see a photo of this dish. The yellow and coral colors set off by the smoky salsa flavor provide a veritable rainbow for your palate.*

Smoked Corn Salsa (recipe follows)
Pico de Gallo (page 153)
4 (6-ounce) salmon fillets
2 tablespoons vegetable oil
1 tablespoon Creole Seafood
   Seasoning (page 156)
1 avocado, cut into 12 slices

Prepare Smoked Corn Salsa; reserve, keeping warm until ready to use. Prepare Pico de Gallo; reserve until needed. Preheat char-broiler or charcoal grill until hot.

Coat fish with oil and season fillets with Creole Seafood Seasoning. Grill fillets on each side about 5 minutes. When turning fish, try to get defined grill marks on at least one side. If fish starts to become too dark, move to a cooler part of grill to finish.

To serve, ladle ½ cup reserved Smoked Corn Salsa onto each dinner plate and top with grilled fish. Sprinkle with reserved Pico de Gallo and 3 avocado slices.

Chef's Tips: Mahi mahi and amberjack are two other excellent choices that go well with this salsa.

Whenever you have the smoker fired up, add a few ears of corn, even some onions and tomatoes. There are now small stovetop smokers available. Make sure that the range-hood system vents to the outside so your smoke alarm doesn't go crazy.

## SMOKED CORN SALSA

Yield: 2½ cups

2 cups freshly cut corn kernels
½ cup small diced yellow onion
2 tablespoons vegetable oil
2 teaspoons finely chopped
   fresh herbs (basil, thyme
   and/or oregano)
2 cups whipping cream
Salt and black pepper to taste

Prepare smoker and smoke corn and onion until slightly softened.

Heat oil in a large skillet over medium-high heat. Sauté corn and onion. When onion is translucent, add herbs and cream. Reduce heat to medium and cook until liquid is reduced by half.

Season with salt and pepper; reserve, keeping warm until ready to use.

Banquet chef Jermaine Brown and Francisco Valles in action

## CRAB CAKES

Yield: 4 servings

*Chef's Note: Crab cakes have been around since the 19th Century in New Orleans. Blue crabs from the Gulf of Mexico are our top choice.*

1 recipe Lemon Beurre Blanc
   (page 155)
1/2 cup vegetable oil, divided
3/4 cup finely chopped onion
3/4 cup finely chopped green
   bell pepper
1/4 cup finely chopped celery
2 teaspoons minced garlic
1 pound jumbo lump crabmeat,
   cleaned and picked over
1 teaspoon Louisiana hot
   pepper sauce
2 teaspoons Creole Seafood
   Seasoning (page 157)
1 tablespoon Worcestershire sauce
2 tablespoons grated
   Parmesan cheese
1 egg, slightly beaten
1/4 cup bread crumbs
2 tablespoons thinly sliced
   green onion
1/2 cup all-purpose flour
Additional jumbo lump crabmeat
   for garnish (optional)

Prepare Lemon Beurre Blanc; set aside and keep warm.

Heat 2 tablespoons oil in a medium skillet over medium-high heat almost to smoking point. Add onion and sauté 1 minute. Add pepper, celery and garlic; sauté until soft. Reduce heat and add crabmeat, hot sauce, Creole Seafood Seasoning, Worcestershire and cheese to vegetables; cook until heated through.

Remove skillet from heat. Add egg, bread crumbs and green onion; blend well. Form mixture into 8 patties and dust with flour. In a large skillet, heat remaining 6 tablespoons oil over medium-high heat. Reduce heat to medium and sauté crab cakes about 3 minutes on each side, or until golden.

Ladle a generous 1/4 cup reserved Lemon Beurre Blanc onto each plate; set 2 cakes on sauce. Optional garnish: sauté crabmeat until heated through and top crab cakes with a generous spoonful.

Chef's Tips: When making crab cakes, avoid over-stirring the mixture — you don't want to break up the crabmeat.

For hors d'oeuvres, make the cakes nickel-sized, lightly dust with flour, and sauté. Serve with a dollop of Ravigote Sauce (page 49) or a tartar sauce. Or use this crabmeat mixture for stuffing.

We top our Crab Cakes with extra jumbo lump crabmeat briefly sautéed and accompanied with fresh jumbo asparagus.

*"The only real stumbling block is fear of failure. In cooking you've got to have a what-the-hell attitude."*
*— Julia Child*

Crab Cakes

## CRAWFISH KACAL

Yield: 6 servings

*Chef's Note: Way back when, the most popular crawfish entrée on our menu was a simple sauté of Creole-seasoned crawfish over angel hair pasta. Bill Kacal, a friend and frequent restaurant guest, asked us to sauté andouille sausage in with his crawfish and pasta. The sausage really pops the flavor out in this dish. We decided several years ago that the andouille addition should become permanent. and christened the dish Crawfish Kacal. It's rewarding to have a guest's request play a vital role in refining our Creole cuisine.*

1 recipe Kacal Sauce (recipe follows)
6 tablespoons unsalted butter, divided
1 cup medium chopped tomato
1 pound angel hair pasta, cooked
Salt and black pepper to taste
2 tablespoons thinly sliced green onion
Boiled whole crawfish for garnish

Prepare Kacal Sauce; reserve and keep warm. Heat 3 tablespoons butter in a large skillet over medium-high heat. Add tomato; sauté. Stir in pasta. Season with salt and pepper. Stir in remaining 3 tablespoons butter.

With a meat fork or tongs, spiral pasta in center of individual bowls. Spoon reserved Kacal Sauce around the pasta; garnish with onion and boiled crawfish.

## KACAL SAUCE

Yield: 6 cups

2 tablespoons vegetable oil
1/2 pound andouille or smoked spicy sausage, sliced 1/4-inch thick and cut into half moons
2 pounds crawfish tail meat
1 tablespoon Creole Seafood Seasoning (page 157)
2 tablespoons Louisiana hot pepper sauce
2 tablespoons Worcestershire sauce
1/4 cup brandy
1/2 cup whipping cream
1 cup cold unsalted butter, cubed

Heat oil in a large skillet over medium-high heat; add sausage and cook until fat is rendered.

126

Crawfish Kacal

Add crawfish and sauté 2 to 3 minutes. Mix in Creole Seafood Seasoning, hot sauce, Worcestershire and brandy. Reduce heat to medium and cook until liquid is reduced by half. Add cream and cook until liquid is reduced by half. Reduce heat to medium-low and slowly add butter, incorporating after each addition.

Check seasoning; adjust it up a notch with Creole Seafood Seasoning. Reserve, keeping warm until ready to use.

Soft-shell crabs

## CRAWFISH ETOUFFÉE

Yield: 4 servings

*Chef's Note: We have the Cajuns to thank for etouffée, a word derived from a French word meaning food that is smothered.*

2 cups Etouffée Base
   (recipe follows)
2 tablespoons vegetable oil
1/2 cup finely chopped onion
1/2 cup finely chopped green
   bell pepper
1/4 cup finely chopped celery
1/2 tablespoon minced garlic
1 pound crawfish tail meat
Creole Seafood Seasoning
   (page 157)
1/2 cup finely chopped tomato
1/2 cup thinly sliced green onion,
   divided
Hot cooked rice
4 whole boiled crawfish
   for garnish

Prepare Etouffée Base; set aside. Heat oil in a large skillet over high heat. Add onion, pepper, celery and garlic; sauté 2 to 3 minutes, or until vegetables soften.

Add crawfish and 1 teaspoon Creole Seafood Seasoning; continue to sauté 2 to 3 minutes. Blend in reserved Etouffée Base and bring to a simmer for 10 minutes. Add tomato and 1/4 cup green onion; adjust seasoning with Creole Seafood Seasoning. Turn off heat and keep warm until ready to serve.

Place a scoop of rice in center of each bowl; surround by Etouffée. Garnish with a whole boiled crawfish and sprinkle each serving with 1 tablespoon of remaining green onion.

**Chef's Tips:  Substitute chicken stock in the Etouffée Base, pan-sear seasoned chicken pieces, and add the same vegetables. Pour the Etouffée Base over the chicken, vegetables and seasonings; cover and bake until chicken is tender. Or, choose medium-sized shrimp for the crawfish.**

## ETOUFFÉE BASE

Brown Roux as needed (page 68)
2 cups fish or vegetable stock
1 tablespoon Louisiana hot
   pepper sauce
2 tablespoons Worcestershire sauce
1 tablespoon Creole Seafood
   Seasoning (page 157)

Prepare Brown Roux; reserve.

In a medium saucepan, bring stock to a boil over medium-high heat. Add hot sauce, Worcestershire and Creole Seafood Seasoning.

Gradually stir in reserved Brown Roux until sauce is a medium thickness. Simmer 20 to 30 minutes; reserve until needed.

Louisiana Shrimp Creole with Risotto Jambalaya Cakes

## LOUISIANA SHRIMP CREOLE

Yield: 8 servings

*Chef's Note: When I began making this dish in the Marine Corps, we used dehydrated shrimp. That version doesn't stand up to the fresh shrimp recipes I learned to cook during my days in New Orleans. Every chef has a variation of Shrimp Creole, but I really believe this version is blue ribbon material.*

Risotto Jambalaya (page 129)

Creole Sauce:

1/4 cup vegetable oil
1 cup finely chopped onion
1 cup finely chopped green
   bell pepper
1 cup finely chopped celery
2 garlic cloves, minced
1 (14.5-ounce) can stewed tomatoes
1/4 cup tomato paste
1 cup shrimp stock or water
4 teaspoons Worcestershire sauce
4 teaspoons Louisiana hot
   pepper sauce
1 1/2 tablespoons Creole Seafood
   Seasoning (page 157)
1 1/2 tablespoons cornstarch
1/2 cup cold water
1/4 cup thinly sliced green onion
2 tablespoons chopped fresh herbs
   (basil, thyme and/or oregano)
3 pounds (16/20 count) shrimp,
   peeled and deveined
1/4 cup Creole Seafood Seasoning
1/4 cup vegetable oil

Prepare Risotto Jambalaya; follow directions to make "cakes;" reserve, keeping warm.

Heat 1/4 cup oil in a large saucepan over medium–high heat. Add onion, bell pepper, celery and garlic; sauté until onion is translucent. Stir in tomatoes and tomato paste; cook 3 minutes. Add stock, Worcestershire, hot sauce and 1 1/2 tablespoons Creole Seafood Seasoning; bring to a boil.

In a small bowl, mix cornstarch and cold water; add to saucepan, stirring while returning mixture to a boil. Remove from heat; add green onion and herbs. Season shrimp with 1/4 cup Creole Seafood Seasoning.

Heat ¼ cup oil in a large skillet over medium-high heat; add shrimp and sauté until cooked through, about 5 to 7 minutes.

Stir shrimp into Creole sauce; serve with Risotto Jambalaya or Risotto Jambalaya cakes.

Chef's Tip: If you buy shrimp in the shell, peel and use the shells to make stock. Sauté shells for a minute; add just enough water to cover shells and simmer about 15 to 20 minutes. Strain stock.

## RISOTTO JAMBALAYA

Yield: 8 cups or 16 cakes

*Chef's Note: The name alone brings to mind fun and color. Match it with Louisiana Shrimp Creole (page 128) to feel as if you're actually dining at 3300 Smith in Houston.*

¼ cup vegetable oil
1 pound andouille or spicy smoked sausage, quartered and sliced ½-inch thick
1 cup finely chopped onion
¼ cup finely chopped celery
¼ cup finely chopped green bell pepper
1 tablespoon minced garlic
2¼ cups Arborio rice
5 cups chicken broth or water, divided
¼ cup Louisiana hot pepper sauce
¼ cup Worcestershire sauce
1 (14.5-ounce) can Cajun or Creole stewed tomatoes

½ cup shredded Parmesan cheese
¼ cup thinly sliced green onion
Creole Seafood Seasoning, (page 157) to taste
¼ cup flour

Heat oil in a large saucepan over medium heat. Add sausage, onion, celery and pepper; sauté until onion becomes translucent. Add garlic and rice; cook 1 to 2 minutes, or until garlic and rice start to brown slightly. Increase heat to medium-high and add 1½ cups broth. Stirring constantly, cook uncovered until broth is absorbed. Repeat procedure with 1½ cups broth and then again with the remaining 2 cups of broth. This will take a total of 15 to 20 minutes, and the rice will still be a little under cooked.

Add hot sauce, Worcestershire and stewed tomatoes; cook 10 to 15 minutes, or until rice is "al dente." Fold in cheese and green onion; season with Seafood Seasoning. Reserve warm until ready to serve.

If making Jambalaya cakes, completely cool risotto on a sheet pan, about 2 hours. Form ½ cup rice mixture into a cake, (hockey puck look). Repeat until all cakes are formed. When ready to serve, dust cakes with flour and sauté in batches in a hot skillet, using ¼ cup oil, until hot.

Chef's Tip: Finished risotto should be tender, yet still a touch "al dente."

## CHIPPEWA SHRIMP

Yield: 4 servings

*Chef's Note: Chippewa Shrimp (chip-uh-wah) was one of the very first dishes I learned to prepare when I started working for the Brennan family at Mr. B's Bistro in 1982. Chippewa is the name of a Louisiana Indian tribe. This is one of my all-time favorite recipes with its incredible taste and preparation ease. We freely admit this entrée isn't a low-fat dish with its generous use of butter, but believe it or not, we use less butter than called for in the original dish. The stone-ground grits are definitely worth the trouble to locate. Just put them to the taste test to savor the difference.*

1 cup Chippewa Butter, divided
    (recipe follows)
4 cups Goat Cheese Grits
    (page 144)
1½ pounds (16/20 count) shrimp,
    peeled and deveined
1 tablespoon Creole Seafood
    Seasoning
½ cup white wine
½ cup brandy

Prepare Chippewa Butter; reserve until needed. Prepare Goat Cheese Grits; reserve and keep warm.

Season shrimp with Creole Seafood Seasoning. Melt ¼ cup reserved Chippewa Butter in a large skillet over medium-high heat; add shrimp and sauté. When shrimp start to turn pink, pour wine over shrimp and stir. Since shrimp give off a lot of natural juices, remove shrimp when about done, 3 to 5 minutes. Keep warm and reduce liquid by half.

After wine and cooking juices reduce by half, return shrimp to skillet and carefully pour in brandy. To flambé, carefully ignite brandy by either tilting skillet towards flame on the range or by lighting with a long, tapered match (flaming is optional). After brandy is cooked off, stir in remaining ¾ cup butter; heat until hot.

To serve, place 1 cup reserved warm Goat Cheese Grits in center of each bowl. Spoon shrimp around grits; drizzle with skillet juices.

Chef's Tips: Sometimes when cooking a large amount of shrimp, excess juices cook out of the shrimp. I recommend cooking no more than 30 at a time in a large skillet. If you increase the size of this recipe, saute shrimp in batches. Reduce the cooking juices before adding shrimp back into skillet.

If you want to flame the shrimp, pour brandy into an area opposite the skillet's handle and carefully ignite with a long taper match. Shake contents of skillet to distribute flames.

## CHIPPEWA BUTTER

Yield: 2 cups

*Chef's Note: Use this version of compound butter to sauté crabmeat or to top grilled salmon and halibut. Create your own flavor and use on baked oysters on the half shell or to baste oven-roasted chicken. Steak houses use a variation called maître d'hôtel butter, a blend of lemon juice, parsley and seasonings that melts on top of sizzling steaks or other meats.*

1 pound salted butter, softened
1½ tablespoons minced garlic
1 tablespoon minced shallots
1 tablespoon finely chopped sun-
    dried tomatoes
1 lemon, zest and juice of
1½ tablespoons minced
    fresh chives
1 tablespoon finely chopped fresh
    thyme
1 teaspoon Worcestershire sauce
1 teaspoon salt
½ teaspoon black pepper

Using an electric mixer beat butter, garlic, shallots, tomatoes, lemon zest, lemon juice, chives, thyme, Worcestershire, salt and pepper in a large bowl until butter is creamy.

Place butter in center of a long sheet of plastic wrap; roll into shape of a log and refrigerate until firm. Will keep up to 1 month, frozen.

130

Chippewa Shrimp

## CARL PUSHES THE ENVELOPE

As senior restaurant manager, I take it seriously when a person tells me they want to be a chef or a manager. If they mean it, I expect them to live like it. I have high expectations, but I'll be right there beside them to help and encourage. Bottomline, don't tell me you want to do it if you're not prepared to go the distance.

One of my most satisfying roles is that of teacher and mentor. Ellen Tipton is living proof. Although an attorney, bank vice president and one of my cooking class students, Ellen revealed she longed to be a pastry chef. I invited her to come work on Saturdays, honing her skills. Instead of tiring of the schedule, Ellen spent four years learning the ropes. She accepted my challenge to create dessert specials, some of which appear in this book. When our Banquet Directorship opened up in 1999, Ellen fought for and won the position. She's now Director of Marketing and offices next to me. Other proud success stories include Chefs Mark Holley, John Moore and Gary Tottis, Sous Chefs Javier Lopez and Jose Arevalo, plus many more.

Chef Carl Walker and his sons Engel and Brandon

## PASTA ELLEN

Yield: 4 servings

*Chef's Note: We originally served this dish as a lagniappe, a "little something extra" presented to guests as a tastebud starter. It is still exceptional as an appetizer. However, the lagniappe became so addictive that customers requested an entrée portion. One of those guests is now our Director of Sales and Marketing, who gave up life as a banker and attorney to help write this cookbook and indulge in the pasta dish named in her honor.*

6 tablespoons unsalted butter, divided
$3/4$ cup button mushrooms, cut into quarters
1 teaspoon finely minced garlic
8 ounces angel hair pasta, cooked
$1 1/2$ cups Lemon Beurre Blanc (page 155), divided
1 cup finely chopped tomato
$3/4$ cup thinly sliced green onion, divided
Salt and black pepper to taste
1 pound jumbo lump crabmeat, cleaned and picked over
2 teaspoons Creole Seafood Seasoning (page 157)
$1/4$ cup grated Parmesan cheese

Melt 4 tablespoons butter in a large skillet over medium-high heat. Add mushrooms and garlic; sauté until mushrooms are softened. Add pasta, ¾ cup Lemon Beurre Blanc, tomato and ½ cup green onion. Stir ingredients to combine and warm through. Season with salt and pepper; keep warm.

Melt remaining 2 tablespoons butter in a medium skillet over medium heat; add crab, taking care not to break up the crabmeat,

and sauté. Add Creole Seafood Seasoning and remaining ¾ cup Lemon Beurre Blanc; cook until heated through.

Place pasta in 4 large bowls; top with crab mixture. Sprinkle each serving with Parmesan and 1 tablespoon remaining green onion.

**Chef's Tip:** If the pasta or crab mixture starts to reduce and threatens to separate, add a splash of dry white wine, water or whipping cream to pull the mixture back together.

Chef Carl giving a cooking demonstration

While I was in the United States Marine Corps I was lucky to work with some gung ho Marines who were passionate about cooking — especially those I was stationed with at Pearl Harbor. One of those guys claimed that his dad made the world's best hush puppies. Of course, I told him my father did. The Marine opened his wallet and pulled out a card that said "Dad's Hush Puppies." I knew when I was whipped. I immediately sent for the family recipe so that I'd be prepared the next time.

The Marines I worked with in Hawaii all understood that a good meal becomes great only when it's a complete package — down to the very last element. Our Brennan's of Houston team also respects that philosophy and focuses on sides and sauces with the same enthusiasm as the main course..

It's not uncommon for a sous chef to spend a day combing the countryside for fresh vegetable sources. We are fortunate the Houston area offers such a bounty. The vegetable recipes we offer — like Maple-Glazed Carrots with Rosemary — can be teamed with nearly any entrée. Our Popcorn Rice earns rave reviews and always pairs well with meats and fish. Check our Source Guide to locate the special rice variety that gives the dish its pop. Not to be overlooked are our dozen variations for mashed potatoes — the most comforting of all Southern food.

accompaniments

Maple-Glazed Carrots
with Rosemary

*Chef's Note: When I was growing up, my parents and grandparents always grew potatoes in their gardens, including interesting heirloom varieties. I always loved mashed potatoes. As a child, there were other root vegetables, turnips and parsnips in the garden which I did not fully appreciate. Today at Brennan's of Houston — and in your kitchen — my "country garden fusion cuisine" builds on basic White Potato Smashers.*

## WHITE POTATO SMASHERS

Yield: Approximately 4 – 5 cups or 6 servings

*Chef's Note: Potatoes vary in moisture content. You may wish to gradually add a little extra half-and-half to your smashers, if you prefer a smoother consistency.*

4 cups peeled white potatoes,
   cut into 1x2–inch chunks
1/2 cup unsalted butter
6 tablespoons half-and-half, warmed
Salt and black pepper to taste

Add enough cold water to just cover potatoes in a large saucepan; bring to a gentle boil. Cook until tender about 15 to 20 minutes. Drain potatoes; leave in pan and stir over low heat about 5 minutes, or until potatoes begin to dry out.

   Add half-and-half and butter; whip until smooth with an electric mixer.

   Season with salt and pepper.

## ROASTED GARLIC SMASHERS

2 medium garlic bulbs, roasted as
   directed in Chef's Tip, below
1 recipe of White Potato Smashers

Add roasted garlic pulp to the basic White Potato Smashers, along with butter and half-and-half, season to taste with salt and pepper. If a stronger garlic flavor is desired add minced fresh garlic to your taste.

   Chef's Tip: To roast a whole garlic bulb, cut tip off flush with top of garlic cloves. Rub bulb with vegetable or olive oil. Wrap in foil and set on rack in preheated 350-degree oven. Bake 30 to 35 minutes, or until cloves are soft and tender. Break bulb apart and squeeze the pulp from the garlic cloves (squeeze from root end of bulb).

## HORSERADISH SMASHERS

1 recipe of White Potato Smashers
3 tablespoons prepared horseradish

Add the horseradish when you add the butter and half-and-half, continue with White Potato Smashers recipe. Peeled fresh grated horseradish root maybe substituted.

## GORGONZOLA AND WALNUT MASHED POTATOES

1 recipe of White Potato Smashers
4 tablespoons Gorgonzola cheese
   or another blue cheese
1 tablespoon chopped fresh herbs
   (basil, thyme and/or oregano)

*Walnut Cream Sauce:*

1 tablespoon olive oil
1/2 cup buttermilk, warmed
2 tablespoons chopped walnuts
1 teaspoon rice wine vinegar
2 tablespoons Gorgonzola cheese

Follow instructions for White Potato Smashers; add the 4 tablespoons of Gorgonzola cheese and fresh herbs after adding butter to basic recipe. Season with salt and pepper.

   Mix Walnut Cream Sauce ingredients together in a small bowl and spoon over potatoes and top with Gorgonzola cheese.

## FENNEL SMASHERS

1 large fennel bulb
2 tablespoons unsalted butter
1 recipe of White Potato Smashers
Splash of Pernod (licorice flavor
   liqueur)

Core and cut off top and fronds from fennel, reserving a few frond tops. Finely chop fennel bulb; put into a colander and thoroughly wash.

Heat butter in a large saucepan; add chopped fennel and sauté just until fennel softens. Add fennel to the uncooked potatoes in the basic White Potato Smashers recipe and continue to follow basic recipe.

Add the optional splash of pernod when adding the butter, season with the salt and pepper and sprinkle top of potatoes with the reserved fennel tops.

## CELERIAC SMASHERS

*Chef's Note: Celeriac dates back to the 1500s when it was discovered that wild celery had a mild but flavorful root.*

2 cups peeled celeriac, cut into 1x2-inch chunks
1 recipe of White Potato Smashers (Reduce the amount of potatoes to 2 cups)

Substituting the celeriac for 2 cups of potatoes, follow the basic White Potato Smashers recipe. I like to garnish with some thinly sliced celery sautéed in butter.

*"Never eat more than you can lift"*
*— Miss Piggy*

## PARSNIP SMASHERS

*Chef's Note: This is the one vegetable that I could not stand when I was young. No longer! We often fry thin slices for parsnip chips, an excellent garnish for Parsnip Smashers.*

2 cups peeled parsnips, cut into 1½-inch pieces
1 recipe of White Potato Smashers (Reduce the amount of potatoes to 2 cups)

Substituting the parsnips for the 2 cups of potatoes, follow the White Potato Smashers recipe.

## TURNIP SMASHERS

2 cups peeled turnips or rutabagas, cut into 1½-inch pieces
1 recipe of White Potato Smashers (Reduce the amount of potatoes to 2 cups)

Substituting the turnips for the 2 cups of potatoes, follow the White Potato Smashers recipe.

Sweet and White Potato Smashers

## COUNTRY BUTTER

Since we lived only a mile-and-a-half from my paternal grandparents' farm, I'd walk or ride my bike to their house daily. My grandma would be working in her strawberry patch — just talking to those plants. They had a wonderful garden every year. I remember Grandpa had trouble with raccoons stealing his "roasneers" or sweet corn as most know it. We set up a trap every night but I don't remember ever catching the varmint.

Grandma also sold butter and eggs. She'd sit Grandpa and me down to churn. We'd work while listening to the St. Louis Cardinals with Joe Torre and Bob Gibson. When CBs were popular, her handle was "Country Butter."

Sous Chefs Randy Evans and Chris Shepherd out at the farm

## BASIC SWEET AND WHITE POTATO SMASHERS

Yield: 5 cups or 6 servings

3 cups peeled sweet potatoes,
   cut into 1x2-inch chunks
2 cups peeled white potatoes,
   cut into 1x2-inch chunks
3 tablespoons unsalted butter
Salt and black pepper to taste
See various additional
   ingredients below

To cook potatoes add enough cold water to just cover sweet and white potatoes in a large saucepan; bring to a gentle boil. Cook until tender, about 15 to 20 minutes. Drain potatoes; leave in pan and stir over low heat about 5 minutes, or until potatoes start to dry out. Add butter, whip until smooth with electric mixer. Season to taste with salt and pepper.

## BROWN SUGAR PECAN SWEET POTATO SMASHERS

1 recipe Basic Sweet and
   White Potato Smashers
3 tablespoons brown sugar
1/4 cup toasted pecan pieces

To cooked potatoes add butter and sugar; whip until smooth with an electric mixer. Stir in pecans and season with salt and pepper.

Chef's Tip: In a buttered casserole, top whipped potatoes with 1 cup miniature marshmallows and 1/4 cup medium chopped pecans. Bake in a 300-degree oven 15 to 20 minutes until marshmallows turn golden brown.

## CINNAMON-Y BOURBON SWEET POTATO SMASHERS

1 recipe Basic Sweet and
   White Potato Smashers
3 tablespoons brown sugar
1/4 cup bourbon whiskey
3/4 teaspoon ground cinnamon

To cooked potatoes add butter, sugar, bourbon and cinnamon; whip until smooth with an electric mixer. Season with salt and pepper.

## ANCHO PEPPER AND CUMIN SWEET POTATO SMASHERS

*Chef's Note: This pepper is a poblano before it is dried to become an ancho.*

1 recipe Basic Sweet and
   White Potato Smashers
2 ancho peppers, seeded
   and minced
1 teaspoon cumin
2 tablespoons brown sugar

While potatoes are cooking, toast cumin (see Chef's Tip following Chili-Fried Gulf Oysters page 25); reserve. To cooked potatoes add toasted cumin, butter and sugar to potatoes; whip smooth with an electric mixer. Season with salt and pepper.

## HONEY-ORANGE SWEET POTATO SMASHERS

1 recipe Basic Sweet and
   White Potato Smashers
4 tablespoons honey
Zest of 1 orange

To cooked potatoes add butter, honey and zest; whip until smooth with an electric mixer. Season with salt and pepper.

## KAHLÚA-SCENTED SWEET POTATO SMASHERS

1 recipe Basic Sweet and
   White Potato Smashers
3 tablespoons dark brown sugar
6 tablespoons Kahlúa

To cooked potatoes add butter, sugar and Kahlúa; whip until smooth with an electric mixer. Season with salt and pepper.

## CANDIED-PECAN SWEET POTATOES

Yield: 4 cups

*Chef's Note: Candied-Pecan Sweet Potatoes, real Southern comfort food.*

5 cups (1/2-inch cubes) peeled sweet
   potatoes
1/4 cup vegetable oil
3 tablespoons unsalted butter
6 tablespoons brown sugar
1/4 cup Spiced Pecans (page 25) or
   substitute toasted pecans
1 tablespoon minced fresh parsley
Salt and black pepper to taste

Preheat oven to 375 degrees. Toss potatoes with oil in an iron skillet or roasting pan. Put into oven and bake potatoes, stirring about every 5 minutes, until just tender, about 15 minutes and lightly browned. Remove from oven and set aside.

Heat butter and sugar in a medium skillet over medium-high heat. Stir until sugar dissolves and starts to turn into a caramel sauce. Add potatoes to sauce and gently stir together. Stir in pecans, parsley, salt and pepper. When potatoes are coated with the caramel mixture and hot; serve.

*Chef's Note: If you have a flavored liqueur such as praline, Kahlúa or something similar, give the potatoes a little splash for additional flavor and character.*

Chef's Tip: The cubed sweet potatoes can be deep-fried at 350 degrees and tossed with the sauce. One-and-a-half pounds peeled and cubed potatoes (5 cups) should fill a 32-ounce measuring cup to the rim.

Chef Carl and his "test for the best" recipe testing team

## MAPLE-GLAZED CARROTS WITH ROSEMARY

Yield: 4 servings

*Chef's Note: Carrots never had it so great. Maple syrup and rosemary add just the right blend of sweetness and flavor.*

3 quarts water
$1/2$ tablespoon salt
I pound baby carrots, peeled
2 tablespoons unsalted butter
6 tablespoons maple syrup or sorghum
2 teaspoons finely chopped fresh rosemary
Salt and white pepper to taste

Bring water and salt to a boil in a large saucepan over medium-high heat. Add carrots and blanch about 4 to 6 minutes; drain and reserve.

Melt butter in a large skillet over medium heat. Add maple syrup and rosemary; simmer about 1 minute. Add reserved carrots and sauté until hot. Season with salt and pepper; serve immediately.

## POPCORN RICE

Yield: 2 cups or 4 servings

*Chef's Note: Imagine rice with the distinct aroma of popcorn! All rice derives its flavor from a naturally occurring substance and in popcorn rice (check our Source Guide page 186), this substance appears in much higher concentrations. We build on this serendipitous rice essence by blending in mushrooms, parsley, cream and cheese. You'll discover why it's one of the ultimate side dishes for a range of entrées.*

2 tablespoons unsalted butter, divided
I teaspoon minced garlic
$1/2$ cup popcorn rice
$1 1/4$ cups tepid or regular tap water
I teaspoon salt
$1/4$ teaspoon black pepper
I cup thinly sliced button mushrooms

1/2 cup whipping cream
1 tablespoon thinly sliced
   green onion
1 tablespoon finely chopped
   fresh parsley
1/4 cup finely shredded
   Parmesan cheese

Heat a medium saucepan over medium heat; add 1 tablespoon butter, garlic and rice. Sauté 2 minutes, but do not let rice brown. Add water, salt and pepper; bring to a boil. Cover and reduce heat; simmer until rice completely absorbs water, about 20 minutes; rice should be fully cooked at this step.

In a small skillet, add remaining 1 tablespoon butter and mushrooms. Sauté mushrooms until tender, about 3 minutes. Immediately add mushrooms to rice mixture. Add cream; cook over low heat 2 to 3 minutes. Fold in onion, parsley and cheese; mix well and serve immediately.

🧑‍🍳 Chef's Tip: We scoop the finished rice into a small cup (dipping the cup into warm water between each serving so the rice doesn't stick to inside of cup), then unmold it directly onto a serving plate for an appealing presentation.

## BROILED TOMATOES

Yield: 4 servings

*Chef's Note: We get rave reviews pairing our Eggs Benedict with this easy vegetable accompaniment. Go for fully ripe tomatoes. If you want to get fancier, simply hollow out tomato halves and stuff them with Creamed Spinach (page 75).*

2 medium tomatoes, cored
   and cut in half crosswise
1 teaspoon Creole Seafood
   Seasoning (page 157)
4 tablespoons grated
   Parmesan cheese
2 teaspoons finely chopped
   fresh parsley

Preheat oven to 375 degrees. Cut a small slice off bottom of each tomato half to make it level. Sprinkle halves with Creole Seafood Seasoning.

Combine cheese and parsley in a small bowl. Dust top of each tomato with cheese and parsley mixture. Place tomatoes on a baking sheet sprayed with nonstick cooking spray. Bake 15 to 20 minutes, or until cheese is melted and tomatoes are cooked through.

## CRAWFISH AND ANDOUILLE STUFFING

Yield: 3 cups

*Chef's Note: This flavor-packed and versatile stuffing helped win honors at the National Pork Cook-Off in Houston.*

1 tablespoon vegetable oil
1 cup chopped andouille or
   smoked spicy sausage
1/2 cup finely chopped onion
1/4 cup finely chopped red bell
   pepper
1/4 cup finely chopped
   poblano pepper
1 tablespoon minced garlic
1 pound crawfish tail meat,
   coarsely chopped
1 tablespoon Louisiana hot
   pepper sauce
1 tablespoon Worcestershire sauce
1 1/2 teaspoons Creole Seafood
   Seasoning (page 157)
2 cups shredded pepper Jack cheese

141

Heat oil in a large skillet over medium-high heat. Add sausage and render fat; drain all but 2 tablespoons of fat from pan. Add onion, bell and poblano peppers and garlic; sauté until onion is translucent.

Add crawfish, hot sauce, Worcestershire and Creole Seafood Seasoning. Sauté until mixture is hot, remove from heat, and fold in cheese. Store stuffing in covered container in refrigerator up to 2 days.

🧑‍🍳 Chef's Tip: Fill chicken breasts with this mixture and stand back for the applause.

## TEXAS CORNBREAD PUDDING

Yield: 8 Servings

*Chef's Note: Texas Cornbread Pudding has been a Brennan's Thanksgiving tradition for the last five years. Whenever we see clean plates, we go by the theory: "If it's not broke, don't fix it." Originally, I wanted an accompaniment to set off our Creole Barbecue Shrimp (page 34). We'd made loads of sweet bread puddings, so I thought it was time for a savory version.*

4½ cups crumbled Homestyle Cornbread (page 145)
1 tablespoon vegetable oil
½ cup finely chopped yellow onion
1½ cups fresh corn kernels, about 3 ears
4 eggs
2 cups whipping cream
1½ cups shredded pepper Jack cheese, divided
Salt and white pepper to taste
1 jalapeño, thinly sliced (optional)

Prepare Homestyle Cornbread; reserve. Preheat oven to 325 degrees. Heat oil in a medium skillet over medium-high heat. Add onion and corn; sauté until onion is translucent. Set aside.

Whisk together eggs and cream in a large bowl. Stir in reserved cornbread, reserved corn mixture and 1 cup cheese. Add salt and pepper; pour into a greased 8x8x2-inch baking pan. Sprinkle top with remaining ½ cup cheese and jalapeño slices if desired.

Texas Cornbread Pudding

Cover pan with aluminum foil and set in water bath (a larger pan of hot water that comes to within ½ inch of top of baking pan). Bake 1½ hours, or until custard is firm in center.

Chef's Tips: Bake the cornbread a day ahead. If you find yourself in a rush, simply use a box mix that will yield the right amount of crumbled cornbread for this recipe. Caution: Please don't overbake! This dish proves to be such a crowd pleaser that you may want to double the recipe. Use a 9x13x2-inch pan and increase baking time slightly.

## CREOLE OYSTER STUFFING

Yield: 4 cups

*Chef's Note: The first time I made oyster stuffing at Commander's Palace, Ella Brennan said, "Where are the oysters?" I got the point. In this recipe there are 3 cups of oysters in the 4 cups of stuffing. Among the multiple dishes we pair with this special filling are our Beef Wellington Creole-Style (page 88-89) and Oyster Cakes and Eggs (page 76).*

¼ cup unsalted butter
2 cups finely chopped onion
1 cup finely chopped celery
1 cup finely chopped green bell pepper
1 teaspoon minced garlic
3 cups shucked oysters, divided
2 tablespoons Louisiana hot pepper sauce
2 tablespoons Worcestershire sauce
2 bay leaves

½ teaspoon salt
1½ tablespoons Creole Seafood Seasoning (page 157)
1 cup plain bread crumbs

Preheat oven to 325 degrees. Heat butter in a large skillet over medium-high heat. Add onion, celery and bell pepper; sauté 3 minutes. Add garlic and sauté 2 minutes.

Coarsely chop half the oysters; reserve whole oysters. Add chopped oysters, hot sauce, Worcestershire, bay leaves, salt and Creole Seafood Seasoning to sautéed vegetables. Simmer 5 minutes; remove from heat. Stir in bread crumbs and reserved 1½ cups whole oysters.

Place stuffing in a greased 8x8x2-inch pan and bake uncovered 45 to 60 minutes. Stir every 15 minutes to break up any crust that forms on top. Discard bay leaves. If you plan to use this stuffing to fill meat, refrigerate at least 2 hours, or until thoroughly chilled.

Chef's Tips: When adding bread crumbs, remember stuffing will lose a fair amount of moisture due to evaporation during baking. Don't add too many bread crumbs!

If you're tempted to use Creole Oyster Stuffing as a side dish, I suggest doubling the recipe. Use a 9x13x2-inch baking pan and increase baking time slightly.

# Food for Thought & Thought for Food

Alex Brennan-Martin professes admiration for anything well-crafted, be it food, architecture or words. You'll find his office complete with a dozen books on witty quotes.

Alex's Aunt Adelaide and Aunt Dottie Brennan festooned their Louisiana homes with positive pearls of wisdom. Taking a note from them, Alex and Chef Carl decorated our Chef's Dining Room with thought-provoking culinary sayings, fun examples of which add to the pages of our cookbook.

## GOAT CHEESE GRITS

Yield: 8 (½ cup) servings

*Chef's Note: While stationed at the Marine barracks in Pearl Harbor, I only served grits as a breakfast cereal. One eventful day, I gave the grits a nice coating of brown sugar. What a mistake! Gunnery Sergeant Springer, who hailed from the Carolinas, gave me a life-changing lesson in just how to serve Southern grits. I've never put sugar on grits again! Now, I add herbs and goat cheese to grits and surround them with Chippewa Shrimp (page 130).*

4 cups cooked stone-ground grits
½ cup whole milk
½ cup crumbled soft goat cheese
4 teaspoons chopped fresh herbs
   (such as basil, thyme or oregano)
Salt and white pepper to taste

Warm grits and milk in a medium saucepan over medium heat; stir to blend. Fold in cheese and herbs. Heat to serving temperature. Season with salt and pepper.

Chef's Tip: Cook grits according to package instructions. These Goat Cheese Grits are a great accompaniment to just about anything you serve. You may say you don't care for grits. That's probably true if you've never tasted antebellum style grits ground on North Carolina granite. Ground-to-order grits must be kept refrigerated. Check our Source Guide (page 186) for ordering information.

## WARM POTATO SALAD

Yield: 4 servings

*Chef's Note: Warm Potato Salad and Chicken-Fried Catfish are a heaven-made match. Warm Potato Salad was a welcome change after we completed recipe-testing. Even after hours of tasting, we still managed to inhale an entire bowl.*

½ cup Mama's Bacon Dressing
   (page 44)
2½ cups potatoes, peeled and diced
   into large chunks
1 tablespoon Creole mustard
1 medium poblano pepper,
   finely chopped
2 tablespoons finely chopped
   yellow onion
¼ cup finely chopped tasso ham
   (or other spicy ham)
1 teaspoon salt
1 teaspoon black pepper

Prepare Mama's Bacon Dressing; keep warm. Boil potatoes; drain and combine in a large bowl with reserved Mama's Bacon Dressing and mustard. Add poblano pepper, onion and ham; toss to combine. Season with salt and pepper. Serve warm.

Chef's Tip: Keep Mama's Bacon Dressing on hand — not only for Warm Potato Salad, but for knockout spinach salads, too. This dish is usually served warm, but refrigerate any leftovers and eat them chilled or reheated.

# Homestyle Cornbread

Yield: 8 to 12 servings

*Chef's Note: Nothing says the South like cornbread. Slather a right-from-the-oven piece with regular or flavored butter. Douse it with honey. Add corn kernels, green chiles or chopped bell peppers to the mix. My granny tossed in a handful of cracklings. We feature it in our Texas Cornbread Pudding (page 143), Smoked Salmon Cheesecake crust (page 37), and even at employee meals.*

1 cup cornmeal
1 cup corn flour (masa harina)
1/2 cup all-purpose flour
6 tablespoons sugar
4 teaspoons baking powder
3/4 teaspoon salt
1 cup whole milk
1/2 cup buttermilk
2 eggs, slightly beaten
5 tablespoons unsalted butter, melted

Preheat oven to 375 degrees. In a large bowl, combine cornmeal, corn flour, all-purpose flour, sugar, baking powder and salt. In a small bowl, blend milk, buttermilk and eggs. Pour liquid mixture over dry ingredients; stir just until dry ingredients are moistened. Stir in melted butter just until incorporated.

Pour batter into an oiled 9x13x2-inch baking pan. Bake 25 to 30 minutes, or until a toothpick inserted in the center comes out clean.

Chef's Tips: Make cornbread the day before if using for cornbread pudding. Nowadays there are mills where you can buy freshly ground cornmeal and corn flour. My wife Rula tested this recipe. When I cut a piece to taste test, I immediately went back for the butter and my dad's homemade maple syrup and ate almost half the pan.

Toast cornbread for a new style of crouton. Use with smoked chicken, turkey or for ham sandwiches.

Chef Carl Walker and his wife Rula

## DECORATING THROUGH THE SEASONS

We want guests to enter 3300 Smith and be wowed. Seasonal imaginations go wild from Valentine's and St. Patrick's Day through Christmas and New Year's Eve.

We deck the Creole halls all year 'round with sparkling confetti, happy balloons, celebration dessert plates, floral kissing balls, chef toque cornucopias, fancy napkins, ice sculptures, candies, gold sealed praline bags and burgundy ribbon striping the tables.

Come Mardi Gras, Brennan's of Houston goes green, gold, and purple with doubloons, parade beads, masks, do rags and costumed diners.

Miniature ornamental pumpkins, baby Indian corn, colorful striated squashes and pheasant feather arrangements mean Thanksgiving's arrived.

December holiday hues appear in cranberry-filled crystal and silver baskets mounded with red and green bell peppers or apples. Guests collect our musical jingle bells as valued favors.

Chef Carl Walker with Chef Emeril Lagasse

## VEGETABLE HASH

Yield: 4 servings

*Chef's Note: Vegetable Hash is an accompaniment you'll find yourself repeating at endless mealtimes. It tastefully sets off our Spiced Pumpkin Seed Chicken, and I would not hesitate to put it under Chef Carl's Peppercorn-Crusted Filet Mignon.*

4 cups potatoes, peeled and cut into medium dice
3 tablespoons vegetable oil
2 Roma tomatoes
10 jumbo spears asparagus, tough ends removed
12 pearl onions
2 tablespoons unsalted butter
1/2 cup sliced mushrooms (oyster, shiitake, button or a combination)
1 tablespoon finely chopped garlic
2 tablespoons finely chopped fresh herbs (such as thyme, oregano and basil)
Salt and black pepper to taste

Preheat oven to 350 degrees. On a sheet pan, toss potatoes in oil; roast 15 to 20 minutes, or until cooked through. Remove from oven and reserve until needed.

Bring 2 quarts of water to a boil in a large saucepan; add 1 tablespoon salt. Have a bowl with about 2 quarts of ice water standing by. Add tomatoes to boiling water and transfer to ice water as soon as skins start splitting. Remove from ice water and set aside.

Next add asparagus to same boiling water and blanch until asparagus just turns bright green and is tender-crisp (about 8 minutes). Transfer to ice water to stop cooking process; drain.

Add onions to boiling water, blanch about 4 to 5 minutes, or until just tender. Transfer to a colander and cool slightly; peel and reserve. Peel, seed and julienne tomatoes; reserve until needed. Cut asparagus into 1-inch pieces; reserve until needed.

Heat butter in a large skillet over medium heat; add onions and sauté 2 minutes to let onions brown slightly. Add reserved asparagus, mushrooms and garlic; cook 3 to 4 minutes, or until mushrooms are tender. Fold reserved potatoes into sautéed vegetables, being careful not to break potatoes. Cook mixture 1 to 2 minutes to heat vegetables thoroughly. Add reserved tomatoes and herbs. Take skillet off heat; season with salt and pepper.

**Chef's Tip:** This is a good use for leftover steamed vegetables, so don't be shy about cooking up your own version of Vegetable Hash, depending on the produce you have on hand and the limits of your creativity.

## DAD'S HUSH PUPPIES

Yield: 10 (2 hush puppies each) servings

*Chef's Note: Dad says these are better if you leave the little bugs in the cornmeal!!*

3 cups vegetable oil
1 1/4 cups yellow cornmeal
1/4 cup all-purpose flour
1 tablespoon sugar
3/4 teaspoon baking powder
1/4 teaspoon baking soda
1 egg
3/4 cup buttermilk
2 dashes Tabasco sauce
1/2 cup finely chopped onion
3/4 teaspoon salt
3/4 teaspoon black pepper
Pinch of cayenne pepper

Heat oil in deep fryer to 350 degrees.

Mix cornmeal, flour, sugar, baking powder and baking soda in a medium bowl. Add egg, buttermilk and Tabasco; mix thoroughly. Stir in onion, salt, black and cayenne peppers.

Gently drop batter by rounded teaspoonful into hot oil. Deep fry several at a time turning over until both sides are golden brown, about 2 to 3 minutes.

Remove with a slotted spoon and drain on paper towels. Repeat with remaining batter. Serve immediately.

147

Brennan's of Houston sign

Chili Corn Sauce
(page 151)

Homemade
Worcestershire
Glaze (page 154)

Roasted Tomatillo Salsa
(page 27)

Ravigote
Sauce
(page 49)

Pontchartrain Sauce
(page 121)

REMOULADE SAUCE
(page 31)

CREOLE SAUCE
(page 128)

CHORON SAUCE
(PAGE 153)

PICO DE GALLO
(page 153)

MARCHANDS
DE VIN SAUCE
(page 154)

## CHAMPAGNE FENNEL CREAM

Yield: 1½ cups

*Chef's Note: A silken finish for Flounder Veronique or another mild-flavored fish.*

1 bulb fresh fennel
   (also called anise)
1 tablespoon vegetable oil
1 cup champagne
1 cup whipping cream
Juice of ½ lime or lemon
1 tablespoon butter
Salt and white pepper to taste

Remove and discard: core at base of fennel bulb, and round area and fronds at its top, saving a few fronds for garnish. Separate enough layers to cut 1-inch julienne strips of fennel to yield ½ cup; reserve. Coarsely chop remaining fennel bulb.

Heat oil in a medium saucepan over medium-high heat; add fennel and sauté 5 minutes, or until fennel starts to soften. Add champagne and simmer until reduced to about ¼ cup. Add cream and simmer until it begins to thicken, about 5 to 7 minutes.

Pour mixture into a blender or food processor; purée until smooth. Strain sauce through a fine mesh strainer and place in a clean medium saucepan. Simmer until sauce is thickened enough to coat the back of a spoon. Squeeze lime juice into sauce; blend well.

Heat butter in a small skillet over medium-high heat; add reserved julienned fennel and sauté until tender; stir into sauce. Season with salt and pepper.

## CREOLE MEUNIÈRE SAUCE

Yield: 1½ cups

*Chef's Note: This brown butter sauce sets off our favorite Pecan Fish to a "T."*

1 cup Veal or Beef Stock (page 69)
½ tablespoon butter, softened
½ tablespoon all-purpose flour
1 tablespoon Worcestershire sauce
1 tablespoon Louisiana hot
   pepper sauce
½ lemon, peeled and quartered
¾ cup unsalted butter, cubed
Salt and black pepper to taste

Prepare stock; reserve. Prepare beurre manié (kneaded butter) by combining ½ tablespoon butter and flour with a fork until thoroughly mixed and it starts to form a ball.

Combine reserved stock, Worcestershire, hot sauce and lemon in a heavy-bottomed, small saucepan. Cook over medium heat until liquid is reduced by half. Add beurre manié, a small piece at a time, to thicken sauce to medium consistency. Simmer on low heat 5 minutes.

Reduce heat to a very low simmer and add butter, a little at a time, until incorporated. Season with salt and pepper. Turn off heat, strain sauce through a fine strainer and keep warm until ready to use.

**Chef's Tips:** Use canned, no-salt beef broth for the stock.

Beurre manié, French for kneaded butter, is used to smooth and finish some sauces.

Broiled fish loves being teamed with Creole Meunière Sauce. When we mound lump crab over broiled fish and lace it with this flavorful sauce, it goes by the name Fish Grieg. Hosts who choose Fish Grieg for their parties have guests eating out of their hands!

Pasta lovers take note! Our chefs like to sauté shrimp or crab with chopped tomato and sliced green onion. Tossing that combination with Creole Meunière Sauce and angel hair pasta before dusting it all with grated Parmesan really rates high on the satisfaction scale.

## SAUTÉED CRAWFISH SAUCE

Yield: 2½ cups

1 tablespoon vegetable oil
1 pound crawfish tail meat
½ tablespoon Creole
   Seafood Seasoning (page 157)
1 tablespoon Louisiana hot
   pepper sauce
1 tablespoon Worcestershire sauce
2 tablespoons brandy
¼ cup whipping cream
½ cup cold unsalted butter, cubed

Heat oil in a large skillet over medium-high heat; add crawfish and sauté 2 to 3 minutes.

Mix in seafood seasoning, hot sauce, Worcestershire and brandy. Reduce heat to medium and cook until liquid is reduced by half. Add cream and cook until liquid is reduced by half. Reduce heat to medium-low and slowly add butter, incorporating after each addition.

Check for seasoning; if needed, add more Creole Seafood Seasoning to give it a little kick. Reserve, keeping warm until ready to use. Sauce is best when served immediately.

Chef's Tip: Use this sauce to embellish grilled fish, a grilled veal chop or a chicken breast and Louisiana Crawfish and Eggs (page 76).

## CHILI CORN SAUCE

Yield: 4½ cups

2 tablespoons vegetable oil
¾ cup julienned onion
¾ cup julienned poblano pepper
¾ cup julienned red bell pepper
1½ cups fresh corn kernels
½ cup tequila
1½ cups whipping cream
1 teaspoon ground cumin
1 tablespoon chili powder
Salt and black pepper to taste

Heat oil in a medium skillet over medium-high heat. Add onion, poblano, red peppers and corn; sauté until vegetables are tender. Deglaze pan with tequila and cook until liquid is reduced by half.

Add cream, cumin and chili powder; cook until reduced enough to coat the back of a spoon. Season with salt and pepper. Reserve and keep warm until ready to use.

Chef's Tips: Imagine this tasty sauce paired with a grilled filet mignon encircled by crispy fried oysters — a slice of Creole heaven!

To make this sauce attractive, it is important to take your time in cutting the onion and peppers. Cut pepper in half, seed it, and then cut into uniform pieces, about ⅛ inch by ⅛ inch by 1 inch. At the restaurant, we even flatten the pepper, remove the membrane and trim the thickness of the pepper to a uniform ⅛ inch.

## JACK DANIEL'S MOLASSES VINEGAR

Yield: ⅔ cup

*Chef's Note: This easy sauce compliments Oatmeal-Crusted Pork Loin and a multitude of other meat and chicken dishes.*

5 tablespoons Jack Daniel's
   Black Label
⅓ cup molasses
7 tablespoons apple cider vinegar
2 tablespoons chilled unsalted
   butter, cut into small pieces
Salt and black pepper to taste

Place Jack Daniel's, molasses and vinegar in a small heavy-bottomed saucepan. Simmer over medium heat until reduced by half, about 10 to 12 minutes.

Whisk in butter one piece at a time until each piece is incorporated into the mixture. Season with salt and pepper; serve warm.

Chef's Tip: If you run out of Jack Daniel's, another Tennessee whiskey will do. If you want to get ahead, make base reduction and add butter to the re-warmed base closer to serving time.

151

# HOLLANDAISE SAUCE

Yield: 2 cups

*Chef's Note: Hollandaise is the staple sauce used as a foundation for numerous variations. Eggs Benedict is the most renowned of our egg dishes to be embellished by Hollandaise Sauce.*

## Clarified Butter

*Method 1:* Put butter into a medium saucepan on the range and slowly cook over medium-low heat to reduce the water. The solids will sink and stick to bottom of the pan. Just be careful they don't burn onto bottom. Pour off liquid "gold" clarified butter.

*Method 2:* Put butter in a warm place (on top of range with oven on) so it just melts and separates. The solids will float to the top so you can skim them off and the water will sink to the bottom. Pour off clarified butter.

**Points to remember or super hints from the Tall Toque!**

1. Don't let yolks scramble at edges of bowl; remove from heat to check and scrape down bowl with a whisk.

2. It's best to have clarified butter too hot (but not bubbling), rather than too cold.

3. Don't let sauce become too thick when adding butter. If it becomes mayonnaise-thick, add 1 teaspoon warm water at a time.

4. Near the end of adding butter, it's okay if mixture starts to thicken since lemon juice and other possible liquids for seasoning and flavor variations are added at the end.

5. Keep an eye on your sauce after it's made. Hold in a warm place, and every once in a while, give it a stir to distribute the heat throughout.

6. As sauce cools, it may thicken. If so, thin with a little warm water.

7. Hollandaise Sauce can be made up to 2 hours in advance. I wouldn't keep it over 4 hours. Discard any leftover sauce — it doesn't reheat well.

1 pound unsalted butter
4 egg yolks
3 tablespoons water
Juice of 1 lemon
5 dashes Tabasco sauce
Salt and black pepper to taste

Clarifiy butter using either Method 1 or 2 above in Chef's Tips. Reserve clarified butter, keeping warm.

Place egg yolks and water in a large stainless steel bowl set over a large saucepan of simmering water. Bottom of the bowl should not touch simmering water in pan.

Whisk yolks until mixture thickens. While whisking, watch sides of the bowl to ensure that yolks aren't cooking along sides of bowl. Every 30 to 45 seconds, remove bowl from heat and scrape down sides of bowl with whisk. If water in the saucepan is at a rolling boil, be very careful

since yolks will cook much faster. After a couple of minutes, when whisk is pulled through the yolks, the volume should be tripled and the bottom of the bowl visible. It should take 2 or 3 seconds for the yolks to run back down into the track. Then it's time to add the clarified butter.

Remove bowl from heat and set in center of a rolled wet towel arranged in a circle on the counter. This will help hold the bowl in place while whisking in clarified butter. Whisk butter constantly (until all is incorporated) while pouring in a slow, steady stream into yolks. If sauce becomes too thick, add 1 teaspoon warm water at a time to thin sauce to desired consistency. The sauce should be a slightly thickened, creamy consistency. Season with lemon juice, Tabasco, salt and pepper.

**Chef's Tips:** Don't cheat yourself by using one of those canned or powdered versions of this sauce. There is a difference! It is harder to prepare, but the taste is worth all of the learning errors you make. Be sure to use a thin wire whisk to make this sauce.

## BÉARNAISE SAUCE

*Chef's Note: Béarnaise Sauce is a Hollandaise Sauce with a tarragon reduction; ideal on grilled meats.*

In a small skillet, bring 2 tablespoons white wine and 2 tablespoons minced fresh tarragon (or 1½ tablespoons dried) to a simmer over low heat, until wine is almost completely reduced. Whisk mixture into Hollandaise Sauce (page 152). Keep warm until ready to use.

## CHORON SAUCE

*Chef's Note: Choron Sauce — my personal favorite — is a Béarnaise Sauce with tomatoes added; use to accompany seafood and meat dishes. The tomato product we like to use is the Creole sauce that is the basis for Louisiana Shrimp Creole (page 128).*

Simmer 1 (14.5-ounce) can Cajun or Creole stewed tomatoes in a small saucepan until most of the juice is evaporated. Cool tomato reduction until just warm. Whisk ½ cup tomato reduction into Béarnaise Sauce. Keep warm until ready to use.

## DILL HOLLANDAISE

*Dill Hollandaise is good to top poached fish, such as salmon.*

Stir 2 tablespoons chopped fresh dill into Hollandaise Sauce (page 152). Keep warm until ready to use.

## PICO DE GALLO

Yield: 1½ cups

*Chef's Note: This title, Spanish for rooster's beak, is derived from how it was eaten many years ago. Pico de Gallo gives a refreshing zing to many dishes. When we make it at the ranch where we hunt, it carries more than just a zing. We fire it up with more jalapeños so that the peppers outweigh the other ingredients. The neighbors just think it's the coyotes howling!*

2 medium Roma tomatoes, chopped
½ cup finely chopped yellow onion
½ jalapeño, seeded and minced
2 teaspoons chopped fresh cilantro
2 tablespoons fresh lime juice
Salt and black pepper to taste

Combine tomatoes, onion, jalapeño, cilantro, lime juice, salt and pepper in a small bowl. Serve immediately or store in covered airtight container in refrigerator up to 2 days.

## MARCHANDS DE VIN SAUCE

Yield: 1 cup

*Chef's Note: The French meaning of this sauce is "wine merchants." When I first started working at Mr. B's with French Chef Jean Chaix, we quickly learned that French terms didn't always translate the way we thought. For example, a classical Marchands de Vin is a reduction of sauce Bordelaise. In Creole country however, it has additional garnishes of mushrooms, ham and a few other touches. Creole cuisine only improves time-honored classics.*

3/4 cup Beef or Veal Demi-Glacé (page 69)
5 tablespoons unsalted butter, divided
1 cup thinly sliced button mushrooms
1/2 cup julienned ham (preferably a spicy ham or tasso ham)
1 tablespoon finely chopped shallots
1 tablespoon finely chopped yellow onion
1 teaspoon minced garlic
1/2 cup red wine
1/2 teaspoon salt
Dash black pepper
Dash cayenne pepper

Prepare Beef or Veal Demi-Glacé; reserve. Heat 1 tablespoon butter in a medium skillet over medium-high heat. Add mushrooms, ham, shallots, onion and garlic; sauté until onion is translucent. Add wine and cook until mixture is reduced by half, about 5 minutes. Blend in reserved demi-glacé; simmer over low heat 8 to 10 minutes.

Whisk in remaining 1/4 cup butter by adding a tablespoon at a time until butter is incorporated and totally melted into the sauce. Add salt, black and cayenne peppers. Keep warm until ready to use.

Chef's Tip:  This sauce is used in preparing Eggs Hussard (page 72) and is paired with grilled meats such as a fillet of beef or veal chops.

## HOMEMADE WORCESTERSHIRE GLAZE

Yield: 2 cups

*Chef's Note: While working as Sous Chef with Executive Chef Emeril Lagasse at Commander's Palace, he introduced me to this rendition of Worcestershire sauce. He developed this special contribution for a New York dinner sponsored by the National Cattlemen's Beef Association. We participated in the event with other well-known chefs including Wolfgang Puck, Jean-Louis Palladin and Stephan Pyles. We use our variation of this sauce to finish dishes such as Texas Bobwhite Quail (page 106).*

1 tablespoon olive oil
2 1/4 cups chopped onion
1 jalapeño pepper, seeded and chopped
2 1/2 tablespoons minced garlic
4 cups white vinegar
2 cups water
2 cups dark corn syrup
1 cup molasses
2/3 cup prepared horseradish
1 lemon, peeled and diced
2 1/2 tablespoons minced anchovies
1 dozen whole cloves
1 tablespoon salt
1/4 teaspoon ground black pepper
1/4 cup unsalted butter, divided

Heat oil in a large saucepan over medium-high heat; sweat onion, jalapeño and garlic until tender. Add vinegar, water, corn syrup, molasses, horseradish, lemon, anchovies, cloves, salt and pepper; bring to a boil. Cook uncovered at a rapid simmer over medium to medium-low heat until mixture is thick enough to coat the back of a spoon.

Strain sauce through a fine mesh strainer into a small saucepan. Cook over low heat to reduce volume of sauce by half, until it reaches a syrupy glaze consistency. Should reduce to 2 cups. Store in covered container in refrigerator up to 4 weeks.

To serve, warm Homemade Worcestershire Glaze until hot. For each 1 cup glaze, swirl in 2 tablespoons butter to finish.

Chef's Tip:  An inspired use of our Worcestershire glaze is an appetizer dubbed Andouille Rudelson, for neighbor and friend, Mike Rudelson. We caramelize onions in a skillet, remove them and then sear andouille sausage in the same skillet. The onions, plus a generous amount of Worcestershire glaze, are returned to the skillet until the entire mixture is heated through. This palate-pleasing concoction is then mounded over our Goat Cheese Grits (page 144).

## LEMON BEURRE BLANC

Yield: 1¼ cups

*Chef's Note: Beurre Blanc is one of the great classics to have in your cooking repertoire. Once you master the basic recipe, then you can orchestrate a version to match your taste and imagination.*

1 lemon, peeled and quartered
1 tablespoon minced shallots
½ cup white wine
1 tablespoon whipping cream
1 cup cold unsalted butter, cubed
Warm water as needed
Salt and white pepper to taste

Combine lemon, shallots and wine in a heavy-bottomed, small saucepan. Cook over medium heat to reduce liquid until it starts to become syrupy and thick. Add cream and heat. Whisk in butter one piece at a time, whisking after each addition. If mixture begins to look too thick, add a few drops of warm water.

When all the butter is incorporated, remove sauce from heat and strain. Season with salt and pepper; always KEEP WARM.

Chef's Tip: If the Beurre Blanc breaks down, simply warm it up, spin in a blender and keep warm until serving time. Or use a hand-held blender that you can put into a sauce to help bring it back together.

## HOT SAUCE BEURRE BLANC

*Chef's Note: The spiciness of Hot Sauce Beurre Blanc lends itself to Jose's Shrimp & Tasso En Brochette (page 32-33), as well as a host of other dishes.*

1 recipe Lemon Beurre Blanc
2 to 4 tablespoons Louisiana hot pepper sauce (Crystal Louisiana Hot Sauce is our favorite)

In the Lemon Beurre Blanc recipe instructions, after combining lemon, shallots and wine and reducing to a syrupy consistency, add 2 tablespoons hot sauce; continue recipe.

When seasoning, add another 1 tablespoon or more hot sauce if you still want to give it more power. "Pow!" as Ella Brennan would say.

## TOMATO TARRAGON BEURRE BLANC

*Chef's Note: Drizzle this one over Chicken Pontalba (page 104).*

1 recipe Lemon Beurre Blanc
1 tablespoon tomato paste
1 tablespoon minced fresh tarragon leaves
Tabasco as needed

In the Lemon Beurre Blanc recipe instructions, after combining lemon, shallots and wine and reducing to a syrupy consistency, add tomato paste and tarragon; continue recipe.

When seasoning, add a couple dashes of Tabasco to pep it up.

## SUN-DRIED TOMATO AND BASIL BEURRE BLANC

*Chef's Note: This is an attention getter for Shrimp-Stuffed Chicken Breast (page 100) and Veal Rib-Eye with Artichokes and Mushrooms (page 95).*

1 recipe Lemon Beurre Blanc
2 tablespoons julienned sundried tomatoes
1 tablespoon chiffonade fresh basil leaves

Add sun-dried tomatoes and basil to Lemon Beurre Blanc, close to serving time, to hold color and flavor of basil.

## FRESH HERB BEURRE BLANC

*Chef's Note: Let your green thumb go wild. The herbs you use can vary from a single herb to a combination. It's your choice! Basil, oregano and thyme form a trio that I really like.*

1 recipe Lemon Beurre Blanc
2 tablespoons minced fresh herbs

Add herbs to Lemon Beurre Blanc, close to serving time, to hold flavor and color.

## TERMS OF ENDEARMENT

We've hosted presidents and heads of state, christenings and weddings, but new visitors to Brennan's of Houston always want to see the room where the famous restaurant scene in *Terms of Endearment* was filmed. Jack Nicholson and Shirley MacLaine will forever be remembered here.

Movie producer Jim Brooks chose Brennan's of Houston for a date scene for the characters played by Jack and Shirley. The lovely, small dining room used in the film is known as the *Terms of Endearment* Room.

Table set for a private party

## CREOLE MEAT SEASONING

Yield: 2½ cups

*Chef's Note: The Spice Girls have nothing on Brennan's of Houston! Creole Meat Seasoning is used in dishes from beef and game to poultry.*

³/4 cup salt
6½ tablespoons finely ground black pepper
4 tablespoons cayenne pepper
9½ tablespoons paprika
7½ tablespoons garlic powder
6 tablespoons onion powder

Place salt, black and cayenne peppers, paprika, garlic and onion in a medium bowl; mix thoroughly.

Store seasoning in a covered container and keep in a cool, dry place up to 6 months.

## SHRIMP BOIL

1 quart water
½ tablespoon Louisiana hot pepper sauce
1½ teaspoons Worcestershire sauce
¼ cup coarsely chopped celery
¼ cup coarsely chopped carrot
¼ cup coarsely chopped onion
½ teaspoon finely chopped garlic
5 teaspoons liquid crab boil
1½ teaspoons black peppercorns
Juice of 1 lemon
1½ teaspoons Creole Seafood Seasoning (page 157)
1½ teaspoons cayenne pepper
2 bay leaves
1 tablespoon salt

Combine all ingredients in a large saucepan. Bring mixture to a boil, reduce heat and simmer 5 minutes. Don't let liquid reduce too much or you may throw off the seasoning. To test seasoning, cook 1 or 2 shrimp first and taste with the Remoulade Sauce; adjust spice in Shrimp Boil accordingly.

## CREOLE SEAFOOD SEASONING

Yield: 3½ cups

*Chef's Note: Our kitchen couldn't function without this essential of all cooking basics. We dust it over shrimp, fish, crawfish and crab, or mix it in flour for extra zip.*

¾ cup salt
6½ tablespoons finely ground black pepper
4 tablespoons cayenne pepper
7½ tablespoons garlic powder
6 tablespoons onion powder
1 cup paprika
½ cup tightly packed dried thyme leaves
7 tablespoons tightly packed dried oregano leaves

Place salt, black and cayenne peppers, garlic, onion, paprika, thyme and oregano in a medium bowl; mix thoroughly. Or, place in food processor and pulse lightly to make a finer mixture.

Store seasoning in a covered container and keep in a cool, dry place up to 6 months.

Chef's Tip: When using a store-bought seasoning, there are definite salt and pepper differences. So remember, you can always add seasonings — but you can't take them out once they are in!

World-famous chefs left to right, Wolfgang Puck, Jean-Louis Palladin, Germaine Swanson, Tim Anderson, Anne Breuer, Iris Burnett, Stephan Pyles, Larbi Dahrouch, Emeril Lagasse, Carl Walker and Michael Foley

Bananas Foster was created decades ago by the Brennan family in New Orleans. Much copied, it has become synonymous with elegant dining. Today, whenever I go to another restaurant that has Bananas Foster on the menu, I question the manager or the waiter about how they came up with the incarnation of the dessert they are serving. I've seen Bananas Foster souffles, bread puddings and countless other adaptations. Of course at Brennan's of Houston we are not immune to tweaking the dessert ourselves. Our version involves serving it with butter pecan ice cream in the winter. In Texas, the pecan is the State Tree so you can never go wrong with pecans served in any presentation or manner. We use the bounty of those trees in many sweets, as well as in main dishes.

Of course, my love for desserts is rooted in my childhood — I have vivid memories of fresh apple, cherry and gooseberry pies and Granny's homemade ice cream. However, Grandpa was satisfied with leftover cornbread crumbled in buttermilk.

Later, while I was stationed at Pearl Harbor, I took every correspondence course the Marines offered and attended courses in international cooking and all levels of cake decorating. I ranked high with my fellow servicemen at the end of a cooking class when I came back to the barracks with a frosted cake tied to my motorcycle.

grand finales

Chocolate Praline
Cheesecake

# BANANAS FOSTER

Yield: 4 servings

*Chef's Note: Bananas shipped to the Port of New Orleans flavored boundless Creole desserts. This star-studded favorite honored Owen Brennan's pal, Dick Foster, who served as vice chairman of the Vice Committee that cleaned up the French Quarter during the 1950s. This show-stopper is justifiably No. 1 in the hearts and appetites of legions of our guests.*

½ cup unsalted butter
1 cup packed brown sugar
6 tablespoons light or dark rum, divided
4 ripe bananas, peeled, sliced lengthwise and halved again into quarters
½ teaspoon ground cinnamon
4 scoops vanilla ice cream

In a flat sauté pan or medium skillet, add butter, sugar and 2 tablespoons rum; cook over medium-high heat while stirring to melt. Add bananas; use a table fork to lightly prick bananas while cooking. Sauté about 1 minute, or until bananas start to soften.

Carefully tilt pan towards you to get top half of pan hot, then remove pan from heat.

Pour remaining ¼ cup rum over bananas. To flambé bananas, carefully ignite rum by either tilting pan towards flame on range or cautiously lighting with a long taper match.

Gently shake flaming pan with one hand and sprinkle cinnamon over flame with other hand. This makes the cinnamon sparkle and glow.

When flames die out, immediately spoon bananas and sauce over ice cream.

Chef's Tips: NEVER, ever pour liquor straight from the bottle into a hot pan. Refrain from even leaning toward the pan to protect yourself from any burns.

While the rum is lit, we sprinkle ground cinnamon from a small spice shaker directly into the flame to produce a Fourth of July sparks effect that is pure food magic! If you want more cinnamon, adjust to taste after the flames subside.

During the December holidays, use butter pecan ice cream to add another tasty element to the festivities.

Bananas Foster

162

Cashew Carrot Torte

## CASHEW CARROT TORTE

Yield: 1 (10-inch) torte
12 servings

*Chef's Note: When one happy guest described this torte as "an adult carrot cake," we knew we had a hit on our hands. You'll be tempted to dab the potent citrus-rum sauce on your pulse points.*

5 eggs
1¾ cups vegetable oil
3 cups grated carrots (peeled before grating)
2 tablespoons grated ginger root (peeled before grating)
¼ cup grated orange zest
2 teaspoons vanilla extract
½ teaspoon almond extract
2¼ cups sugar
1 teaspoon cinnamon
1¾ cups toasted chopped cashews
2 cups unsifted all-purpose flour
2½ teaspoons baking powder
1 teaspoon salt
Rum Sauce, divided (recipe follows)
Toasted chopped cashews for optional garnish

Preheat oven to 325 degrees. Butter and dust with flour a 10-inch layer cake pan with 3-inch sides; set aside.

In a large bowl, whisk eggs, oil, carrots, ginger, zest, vanilla and almond extracts until well combined. Add sugar, cinnamon and cashews to carrot mixture; blend well.

Sift together flour, baking powder and salt; add to batter and mix well.

Pour batter into prepared pan. Bake 1¼ hours, or until springy in center and a knife or toothpick inserted into the center of the cake comes out clean.

Prepare Rum Sauce; keep warm. After cake cools slightly, unmold onto a large plate.

Use a toothpick to poke holes all over top of cake.

Saturate cake with ½ cup reserved Rum Sauce by slowly pouring sauce over top; reserve remainder for garnish.

To serve, heat remaining 1¼ cups sauce slightly over medium heat in a small saucepan. Pour into a small pitcher to accompany torte. May also garnish torte with cashews. Cake freezes well.

Chef's Tip: Go nuts! We have successfully and deliciously substituted walnuts, pecans or macadamia nuts for the buttery cashews in this recipe.

## RUM SAUCE

Yield: 1¾ cups

½ cup granulated sugar
1 cup packed brown sugar
½ cup lime juice
½ cup dark rum

In a small saucepan, combine granulated and brown sugars, lime juice and rum.

Cook over medium heat until sugars dissolve; remove from heat.

Keep warm until needed for pouring over torte. Reheat remainder at time of serving.

*"I hate people who are not serious about their meals."*

*— Oscar Wilde*

"Mama" Florence Gibson.

## MAMA FLORENCE'S CARROT CAKE

Yield: 1 (10-inch) 3-layer cake

*Chef's Note: Mama Florence was extremely special to our restaurant family. She originated this towering cake in 1967 — ever a favorite through the decades. When the holidays arrived each year, you could bet Mama was busy making carrot cakes to go. I wanted Mama to be photographed for this book making one, but evidently God needed her more to start making cakes for the angels in heaven.*

3 cups unsifted all-purpose flour
3 cups packed brown sugar
3 teaspoons cinnamon
3 teaspoons baking soda
1³/4 cups vegetable oil
6 eggs
1¹/2 tablespoons vanilla extract
1¹/2 cups peeled and grated carrots
Mama Florence's Carrot Cake
   Frosting (recipe follows)
1¹/2 cups toasted pecan pieces for
   garnish (optional)

Preheat oven to 350 degrees.

In a large bowl, stir together flour, sugar, cinnamon and baking soda.

Add oil, eggs and vanilla to the dry ingredients.

Using a hand mixer, slowly mix ingredients until batter is smooth. Slowly stir in carrots.

Pour into a well-oiled 10-inch layer cake pan with 3-inch sides. Bake 45 minutes, or until a knife or toothpick inserted in the center comes out clean.

Cool cake completely before slicing and frosting.

Prepare Mama Florence's Carrot Cake Frosting; refrigerate until needed.

Slice cake into 3 equal layers using a serrated knife. Spread about ³/4 cup of reserved Mama Florence's Carrot Cake Frosting on the bottom layer. Place middle layer on top of frosting and spread ³/4 cup frosting over middle layer. Stack top layer over frosting. Finish icing sides and top of cake with remaining frosting. If frosting becomes too soft when covering sides of the cake, refrigerate cake and frosting for a few minutes prior to completion.

Apply pecans around the sides of cake for a special garnish.

Chef's Tip: You may have to level off the top of the cake before dividing it into 3 layers. The excess you cut off makes for special snacking! If you have room, place the cake in your freezer 20 to 30 minutes before you begin icing. When frosting sides of the cake, remember to work with chilled frosting.

## MAMA FLORENCE'S CARROT CAKE FROSTING

Yield: 5 cups, enough to frost 1 (10-inch) 3-layer cake

2 (8-ounce) packages cream
   cheese, softened to room
   temperature
¹/2 cup unsalted butter, softened
2 teaspoons almond or vanilla
   extract
2 pounds powdered sugar
1 cup coarsely grated carrots
   (optional)

Using an electric mixer, beat cream cheese, butter and almond extract in a large bowl until mixture is fluffy. Slowly add sugar and blend on slow speed until smooth.

Scrape down sides of bowl and mix until smooth. Add carrots for color and flair.

Refrigerate frosting 1 to 2 hours prior to icing cake or other dessert.

Chef's Tip: A countertop mixer is ideal for making the Carrot Cake and creamy frosting.

Mama Florence's Carrot Cake

## BAKING

My first real customers bought the cakes and pies I made for school fund-raisers. As high school sophomores, we decided we were going somewhere "big" on our "senior trip." I began baking for bake sales – and getting compliments. And my class of 24 spent an entire week in Washington D.C.

It was in the U.S. Marine Corps, though, where I really developed my baking skills. I took all the classes the Corps offered and one November 10th I made the Marine Corps' birthday cake that needed four Marines to carry it.

## CHOCOLATE CHIP PISTACHIO BISCOTTI

Yield: 32 biscotti

*Chef's Note: Before heading off to study pastry abroad, Pastry Sous Chef Laura Crucet whimsically garnished a variety of taste treats with sensational biscotti. The cinnamony dough alone makes this recipe a world class snack. With biscotti around, I don't have to worry about that old myth "Never trust a skinny chef!"*

1/2 cup unsalted butter
1/2 cup packed brown sugar
1/2 cup granulated sugar
2 eggs
2 cups all-purpose flour
1 1/2 teaspoons baking powder
1 teaspoon ground cinnamon
Pinch of salt
1 cup shelled pistachios
1 cup chocolate chips

Using a hand mixer, beat butter, brown and granulated sugars in a large bowl until light and fluffy.

Slowly add eggs, beating until well combined.

Sift together flour, baking powder, cinnamon and salt. Add to batter and mix to form a stiff dough.

Fold in nuts and chocolate chips using a wooden spoon.

Form dough into two slightly flattened logs, approximately 12x2x2 inches. Cover with plastic wrap. Chill dough in refrigerator at least 2 hours.

Preheat oven to 350 degrees. Unwrap logs and bake on a parchment-lined sheet pan 25 to 30 minutes, or until slightly firm.

Cool biscotti completely, about 45 minutes.

Again, preheat oven to 350 degrees. Cut loaves diagonally into 3/4-inch slices and place cut side down on same baking sheet.

Bake 10 to 15 minutes, or until biscotti slices are dry.

When completely cooled, store in an airtight container.

**Chef's Tip:** It's much easier to cut the biscotti into slices if you use a serrated knife.

## LEMON RAISIN SCONES

Yield: 12 (2-inch) round scones

*Chef's Notes: Another former Pastry Chef Melissa Piper Reilly wowed us at weekend brunches with these citrusy scones. Scones originated in Scotland. The name derived from the "Stone of Destiny," where Scottish kings were crowned. Originally they were an oat-based quick bread, cooked on a griddle and cut into triangular shapes.*

2 cups all-purpose flour
1/3 cup sugar
2 teaspoons baking powder
Pinch of salt
1/3 cup cold unsalted butter, cubed
1 egg, beaten
1/2 cup whipping cream
1 tablespoon lemon extract
1 cup golden raisins
1 tablespoon lemon zest
2 tablespoons sugar (optional)

Preheat oven to 375 degrees.

In a large bowl sift together flour, sugar, baking powder and salt.

Add butter and mix with a pastry cutter until coarse crumbs form.

In a small bowl, whisk together egg, cream and lemon extract.

Add egg mixture, raisins and zest to flour mixture, stirring just until combined.

Knead dough gently on a lightly floured surface; do not over handle.

Roll out to ½-inch thickness on a lightly floured surface. Cut scones into 2-inch rounds or other desired shapes.

Place on a baking sheet lined with parchment paper or lightly sprayed with nonstick cooking spray.

Sprinkle top of scones with sugar, if desired.

Bake 15 minutes, or until lightly browned. Serve warm.

Chef's Tip: Make these scones in a smaller size if serving them for tea or snacks. Be sure to use a shorter baking time. Alternatives to golden raisins are regular raisins, currants or dried fruits like chopped apricots, blueberries or cherries.

## MOLASSES SUGAR COOKIES

Yield: 4 dozen

*Chef's Note: These cookies remind me of my childhood when my maternal grandfather, Jake Moyer, made his own sorghum molasses. He was known far and wide for the supreme quality of the cane he selected. (See photo page 134.) Bottled under his label, the sweet sorghum became extra special during World War II when sugar was rationed.*

*Our Molasses Sugar Cookies are such a hit with longtime kitchen manager Thomas Franklin that he would do anything for an endless supply. The cookies have to be kept under lock and key from the chefs and staff alike.*

¾ cup vegetable oil
¼ cup molasses
1 teaspoon vanilla extract
1 egg
1½ cups sugar, divided
2 cups sifted all-purpose flour
2 teaspoons baking soda
½ teaspoon salt
1½ teaspoons ground cinnamon
½ teaspoon ground cloves

Mix oil, molasses, vanilla, egg and 1 cup sugar thoroughly in a large bowl with an electric mixer.

Sift together flour, baking soda, salt, cinnamon and cloves.

Add dry ingredients to molasses mixture and combine well.

Cover dough with plastic wrap and chill at least 3 hours or overnight.

Preheat oven to 375 degrees.

Put remaining ½ cup sugar into a shallow bowl. Form 1-inch balls of dough and roll in sugar.

Place balls 2 inches apart on parchment paper-lined baking sheet. Bake 8 to 10 minutes — do be careful not to over-bake. Cookies will appear soft, but will firm after cooling.

Cool thoroughly on rack; store in airtight container.

Chef's Tips: We use a scoop to shape uniform 1-inch balls of this dough.

These crushed cookies make a taste-filled base for a pumpkin cheesecake crust or as a garnish for coffee ice cream.

## PECAN BOURBON BALLS

Yield: 20 (1-inch) cookies

*Chef's Note: I made my fair share of Pecan Bourbon Balls during my days at Commander's Palace. Dick Brennan, Sr. said they were so potent that people would pack them in their pockets for a little hit of bourbon here and there.*

2½ cups crushed vanilla wafer crumbs
1½ cups sifted powdered sugar, divided
1 cup finely chopped pecans
3 tablespoons corn syrup
⅓ cup bourbon

Combine crumbs, 1 cup sugar and nuts in a large bowl.

Stir in corn syrup and bourbon; form into 1-inch balls and refrigerate.

Roll balls in remaining ½ cup sugar.

Store in covered container at room temperature up to 1 week.

Chef's Tips: If you don't have vanilla wafers, use chocolate wafers or chocolate chip cookies.

Have you ever sampled a Cake Truffle? If you have a leftover unfrosted cake, pulse it in the food processor to form crumbs. Follow the Pecan Bourbon Ball recipe using cake crumbs instead of cookie crumbs to form cake balls and dip into a coating of semisweet, milk or white chocolate for another scrumptious dessert.

## CHEF'S TIPS FOR MAKING NEW ORLEANS-STYLE PRALINES

The ingredients are simple enough. It's the cooking procedure that's tricky.

Use a heavy whisk or wooden spoon for stirring.

The more you stir to eliminate sticking, the lighter in color the pralines. Some caramelizing is good. It's the dark specks that come off the bottom that are bad. If you notice specks in your mixture and don't want speckled pralines, carefully transfer the hot mixture to a new pan to keep from starting over. Test small ones — be careful because the caramelized sugar is very hot and sticky. If all else fails, we will be happy to mail them to you. We make about 800 daily and still blow it occasionally. Don't be too hard on yourself if they're not perfect the first time.

## NEW ORLEANS-STYLE PRALINES

Yield: 4 dozen

*Chef's Note: Our pralines (prah-leens) are: (1) a sinfully creamy confection of sugar, cream and chopped pecans; (2) always found in large quantities at the front door; (3) typically transported in the hands and pockets of Brennan's patrons (Note: always for "some-one else"); (4) believed by those who consume them to have a very low calorie content; and (5) commonly referred to as "pray-leens" in Texas.*

1 quart whipping cream
1 pound (2 cups) granulated sugar
1 tablespoon light corn syrup
1 1/2 cups medium chopped pecans
Zest of 1 medium orange (optional)

Line 3 cookie sheets, preferably with parchment paper but wax paper will work. Also have dessert spoons close by to spoon the pralines onto parchment paper when it's time.

In a large heavy saucepan, slowly simmer cream, sugar, corn syrup and orange zest over low heat. As cream mixture simmers, be careful of boil-over in the early stages. Let mixture reduce, stirring occasionally.

When cream mixture first starts to stick to bottom of pan, you need to stir almost continuously until done. As mixture reduces and the sugar starts to caramelize, the mixture becomes thicker and begins to turn light brown in color.

When mixture reaches the soft-ball stage of 240 degrees, stir in pecans. Continue stirring while looking for the point when mixture starts to pull away from sides of the pan.

Drop a small amount (size of a quarter) onto a lined cookie sheet. Look quickly to see if the praline runs out flat or holds a nice rounded top shape and if praline has a dull looking appearance. Also, the mixture shouldn't have an oily look while in the saucepan; that means the mixture cooked too long.

When ready, the mixture should be close to a firm-ball stage of 248 degrees. However, don't depend entirely upon the candy thermometer.

Use two dessert spoons to spoon out the pralines onto lined cookie sheets. Use one spoon to dip up the hot mixture and the other one to push it off onto the paper.

If you've hit it just right, you should be able to pick up a delicious praline in about 30 minutes. It should appear dry and not be chewy. If after a couple of hours you can't pick one up, leave them in a cool dry area on the pans for a day or maybe two so they will dry out.

When ready, transfer to an airtight container and store up to 1 week or ship off to your friends.

New Orleans-Style Pralines

## GRAND MARNIER CRÈME BRÛLÉE

Yield: 6 (1-cup) servings

*Chef's Note: Jamie Shannon, executive chef at Commander's Palace and a respected friend, shared his unique method of baking crème brûlée — not in a custard cup, but spread out on a shallow soup plate. When I attempted this presentation in Houston, I was met with initial skepticism. Over time, diners became accustomed to our plated brûlée and now relish the extra crunchy topping on the surface.*

1 quart whipping cream
1/2 cup sugar
1/2 cup Grand Marnier
1 vanilla bean, split and scraped
10 egg yolks
1 cup raw sugar
1 1/2 cups fresh berries for garnish
Mint sprigs for garnish

Preheat oven to 225 degrees

In a medium saucepan, bring cream, sugar, Grand Marnier and vanilla bean to a simmer, but don't allow to boil.

Remove from heat and slowly whisk 1 cup of cream mixture into egg yolks in a large bowl. This step is referred to as "tempering" the eggs.

Slowly add remainder of cream mixture to yolks; then strain custard mixture through a fine mesh strainer.

Pour 1 cup of custard mixture into each of six ovenproof soup plates. The idea is to bake the custard in a more shallow and wider dish or plate.

Bake custard 20 to 30 minutes, or until center is set. Depending upon the depth of dish you use, time will vary.

After cooling and before serving, sprinkle top with a light coating of raw sugar. Caramelize sugar with a propane torch and repeat twice. We generally do 2 to 3 coatings of sugar.

Garnish top with fresh berries and a mint sprig.

Chef's Tips:  In the Brennan's of Houston kitchen, Crème Brûlée is baked on a 10-inch ovenproof plate. An ovenproof soup plate works equally well.

To caramelize the top of the custard, we use a propane torch for top results. Treat yourself to a mini-torch at your local hardware or kitchen store for a unique addition to your kitchen equipment. When using the torch, keep it moving back and forth so that you don't over-caramelize one spot.

We use turbinado raw sugar which has coarse, blond colored crystals and a slight molasses flavor. This larger-grained sugar supplies the extra crunch we're striving for.

## CRÊPES FITZGERALD

Yield: 6 servings

*Chef's Note: Entire generations of customers have marked momentous occasions here feasting on Crêpes Fitzgerald. We criss-cross two rolled crêpes, splash them with a warmed berry glaze, and pair them with chocolate-tipped strawberries for a dessert that is almost too pretty to eat.*

12 Sweet Crêpes (recipe follows)
Cream Cheese Filling
   (recipe follows)
3 cups fresh strawberries, hulled,
   quartered and divided
1/2 cup sugar, divided
1/4 cup unsalted butter
1/2 cup Grand Marnier
12 chocolate dipped strawberries
   for garnish (optional)
Mint sprigs for garnish (optional)

Prepare Sweet Crêpes; reserve.

Prepare Cream Cheese Filling; reserve. Lay crêpes out flat with golden side down. Place 3 tablespoons reserved Cream Cheese Filling in center of each crêpe. Take a touch of the filling and place at the 6 o'clock edge of the crêpe. Starting at the 12 o'clock edge, roll up crêpes; reserve in refrigerator.

To make strawberry sauce, purée 1 cup strawberries with 1/4 cup sugar; reserve.

Slowly melt butter in a large skillet over medium heat.

Add remaining 1/4 cup sugar and strawberries to skillet; heat until sugar dissolves. Add reserved strawberry sauce and cook until strawberries start to soften.

Crêpes Fitzgerald

Place rolled crêpes in skillet; reduce heat to low and spoon some of the sauce over the crêpes.

Remove skillet from heat to add Grand Marnier. To flambé sauce, carefully ignite liqueur by either tilting skillet towards the flame on range or by cautiously lighting with a long tapered match.

When the flame goes out, quickly and carefully remove crêpes to individual plates, criss-crossing two on each plate. Divide strawberry sauce among crêpes on each plate.

Garnish each plate with 2 chocolate dipped strawberries or a sprig of mint.

**Chef's Tips:** Always use extreme caution when adding liqueur to a heated pan. NEVER pour alcohol straight from the bottle into a hot pan. Protect yourself by not even leaning in the direction of the pan.

In making crêpes, many times the first crêpe becomes a test crêpe, so don't be discouraged if your first one fails to be perfect. If the cooked crêpe is a little difficult to turn, simply run a small knife around the edge to loosen the crêpe.

Crêpes freeze well; put a square of waxed paper between each crêpe and store in a zip-locking bag. Will keep 1 month in the freezer.

## SWEET CRÊPES

3/4 cup unsifted all-purpose flour
1/2 tablespoon sugar
Pinch of salt
1 cup milk
3 eggs, slightly beaten
1 teaspoon vanilla extract
Vegetable oil as needed

Combine flour, sugar and salt in a medium bowl.

Combine milk, eggs and vanilla in a small bowl.

Add liquid ingredients to dry ingredients; whisk until smooth.

Strain crêpe batter through a fine mesh strainer; refrigerate batter at least 30 minutes before making crêpes.

Brush an 8-inch non-stick skillet with oil; heat over medium-high heat.

Pour 2 tablespoons batter into skillet, rotating and tilting to distribute evenly, covering entire bottom of pan.

Cook 1 minute, or until golden and set; flip crêpe over and cook other side until lightly golden. Place crêpes between sheets of wax paper and stack.

Oil skillet as needed and repeat until all crêpes are made; refrigerate until needed or tightly wrap and freeze up to 1 month.

*Cream Cheese Filling:*

1 (8-ounce) package cream cheese,
   regular or low-fat, softened to
   room temperature
1 tablespoon grated orange zest
1 tablespoon Grand Marnier or
   other orange-flavored brandy
2 tablespoons sugar

In a food processor combine cream cheese, zest, Grand Marnier and sugar; blend until smooth. Reserve until needed.

## WHITE CHOCOLATE BREAD PUDDING

Yield: 9 servings

*Chef's Note: White Chocolate Bread Pudding has achieved celebrity status at Brennan's of Houston. In a sugarholic's world, it contains the four basic food groups: silken white chocolate custard, white chocolate shavings, dark chocolate shavings and a rich, smooth white chocolate sauce.*

3/4 loaf day-old French bread
1 1/2 cups half-and-half
1 1/2 cups whipping cream
2 eggs
5 egg yolks
6 tablespoons sugar
2 teaspoons vanilla extract
6 ounces white chocolate, melted
1 1/2 cups White Chocolate Sauce
 (page 173)
Dark and white chocolate
 shavings for garnish (optional)

White Chocolate Bread Pudding

Preheat oven to 400 degrees.

Remove crusts and cut bread into 1-inch thick slices. Cut enough bread slices to cover the bottom of an 8x8x2-inch pan. Toast bread in oven just until it dries out slightly and starts to turn a little golden; set aside for later use.

Heat half-and-half and cream in a medium saucepan over low heat until it just comes to a simmer. BE CAREFUL of a boil-over.

In a large bowl, beat eggs with egg yolks and sugar just enough to mix. Whisking continuously, pour hot cream mixture in a slow steady stream into yolk mixture; once yolks are hot, you can pour hot cream in a little faster. Blend in vanilla extract.

Scrape melted chocolate into same large bowl and slowly whisk cream mixture with chocolate.

Place a layer of toasted bread in baking pan; strain custard into baking pan, covering bread. Allow to stand 1 hour to let bread absorb custard, turning bread after 1/2 hour so that both sides absorb custard mixture.

Prepare White Chocolate Sauce; reserve, keeping warm until needed.

Preheat oven to 350 degrees.

Place baking pan into another larger pan. Cover baking pan

with aluminum foil. Pour hot water into larger pan to surround and come three-fourths of the way up sides of pudding pan. Bake about 1 1/2 hours. Check every 15 minutes after first 45 minutes, or until set and a knife inserted in center comes out clean. As you check, pull foil back carefully, then re-cover.

Remove from oven and water bath; uncover and cool slightly. When ready to serve, run a knife around edge of pan to loosen; cut into 9 pieces.

Unmold each piece carefully with a spatula onto a dessert plate.

Drizzle warm bread pudding with White Chocolate Sauce. Scatter dark and white chocolate shavings over top of each serving, if desired.

If serving later or the next day, let bread pudding cool about 1 hour, cover and refrigerate. Warm pudding before serving in microwave or place number of portions needed onto a baking sheet, sprayed with nonstick cooking spray and heat in 350-degree oven until heated through. Some like it chilled — especially in the middle of a hot Texas summer. Reheat sauce and serve, per instructions above.

Chef's Tips: When melting chocolate, use a clean dry bowl set over a saucepan of barely simmering water. Stir chocolate every couple of minutes with a rubber spatula scraping the bottom and sides to mix in. Chocolate can burn over hot water if it gets too hot and isn't stirred. To melt 6 ounces of white chocolate easily, break pieces into a glass measuring cup and microwave on 50-percent power about 2 to 2½ minutes. It won't melt into a pool. When done, stir to smooth.

## WHITE CHOCOLATE SAUCE

Yield: 1½ cups

6 ounces white chocolate,
   finely chopped
³/4 cup whipping cream

Put chocolate into a medium metal bowl.

In a heavy-bottom medium saucepan, bring cream to a boil. Pour over chocolate in bowl.

Let mixture rest 5 minutes; whisk until smooth and serve.

Cover with plastic wrap and refrigerate until needed. To serve, return to a warm temperature over low heat.

Chef's Tip: The better quality the white chocolate, the better the dessert.

## CREOLE BREAD PUDDING

Yield: 8 to 12 servings

*Chef's Note: Mama Florence, "Recipe Queen Extraordinaire," perfected our easy rendition of this Louisiana dessert staple. Place a Texas-size portion of this "best ever" pudding in a pool of lip-smacking Whiskey Sauce and you've got comfort food for your soul.*

3 cups packed brown sugar
2 teaspoons ground cinnamon
½ teaspoon ground nutmeg
5 eggs, slightly beaten
I quart milk
2 cups whipping cream
5 teaspoons vanilla extract
14 (1-inch thick) slices day old
   French bread
I cup raisins
I½ cups pecan pieces
Rye Whiskey Sauce (page 175)

Preheat oven to 300 degrees.

In a large bowl, blend sugar, cinnamon and nutmeg. Whisk in eggs, milk, cream and vanilla.

Tear bread slices into big, bite size pieces; place in a lightly buttered 9x13x2-inch pan.

Pour custard mixture over bread and allow to soak until soft, about 1 hour. Stir raisins into pudding; top with nuts.

Bake uncovered 1½ hours.

Prepare Rye Whiskey Sauce; reserve, keeping warm until needed.

Scoop bread pudding into individual bowls and top with reserved Rye Whiskey Sauce.

Chef's Tips: This is an ideal way to use day-old French bread!

To keep spices from clumping together and floating to top of the egg mixture, combine cinnamon and nutmeg with sugar before adding liquid ingredients.

As a bonus, both the Bread Pudding and Rye Whiskey Sauce can be made one to two days in advance. When reheating sauce, don't curdle the egg yolks by using too high a temperature!

I have done numerous versions of bread pudding — from peach and blueberry (for my friend Gary Jordan, of Pikes Peak Outfitters in the Colorado mountains) to savory roasted garlic bread pudding with escargots. I use a custard base of 5 to 9 eggs per quart of cream, depending upon the amount of custard desired.

## CREOLE BREAD PUDDING SOUFFLÉ

Yield: 4 servings

*Chef's Note: Royally dubbed "The Queen of Creole Desserts," Creole Bread Pudding Soufflé became the dessert that rivals Bananas Foster. Picture cinnamony Creole Bread Pudding reincarnated as a puffy cloud that floats to your table. When the waiter cracks open the soufflé crown to pour in a cascade of spirited whiskey sauce, you'll hear the angels sing.*

Rye Whiskey Sauce (page 175)
3 cups baked Creole Bread
    Pudding (page 173)
8 egg whites
10 tablespoons sugar

Powdered sugar in a shaker to sift on top for garnish

Prepare Rye Whiskey Sauce; reserve, keeping warm.

Preheat oven to 375 degrees. Butter 4 (²/₃-cup) ramekins and sprinkle insides with sugar; set aside.

Slightly warm bread pudding to make it easier to mix.

Put bread pudding into a large bowl and break apart with a large serving spoon.

Using an electric mixer, in a clean, dry mixing bowl, add sugar gradually, until a stiff, glossy meringue forms.

Fold one large spoonful of meringue into bread pudding to lighten mixture. Loosely fold remaining meringue into pudding.

Spoon mixture into prepared ramekins. Place a more dense proportion of bread pudding on bottom. Working to the top of ramekin, use a fluffier proportion of meringue. Heap mixture about 1½ inches above the rim and round off the crown using a large spoon.

Bake 15 to 20 minutes.

Upon removing soufflés from oven, dust tops with powdered sugar.

When presenting soufflés at the table, open crown of each soufflé with a spoon and pour in some reserved Rye Whiskey Sauce.

Serve remaining sauce on the side.

**Chef's Tips:** Make Creole Bread Pudding a day ahead.

174

"Spoons," a sampling of five trademark desserts, our New Orleans-Style Praline and a mini Creole Bread Pudding Soufflé

When whipping egg whites, be sure the bowl is free of any oily residue. If you have any doubts, rinse the bowl out with a little white vinegar.

## RYE WHISKEY SAUCE

Yield: 2½ cups

*Chef's Note: If Creole Bread Pudding Soufflé is the "Queen of Creole Desserts," then our intoxicating Rye Whiskey Sauce is the "King of Creole Dessert Sauces."*

2 cups whipping cream
9 tablespoons sugar
1½ tablespoons cornstarch
2 tablespoons cold water
2 egg yolks
¼ cup rye whiskey

Stirring occasionally, heat cream and sugar in a heavy-bottomed medium saucepan over medium-high heat until mixture begins to boil.

Mix cornstarch and cold water in a small bowl until smooth; slowly whisk into simmering cream. Simmer 2 to 3 minutes.

Put yolks into a stainless steel bowl; whisk. Temper yolks by slowly whisking 1 cup hot, thickened cream mixture into yolks. Return yolk mixture to hot cream mixture, whisking in slowly. After mixture is whisked together, cook over medium-low heat until mixture reaches 140 degrees. Remove from heat and pour through a fine mesh strainer.

Add whiskey, adjusting to taste, and keep warm until ready to use.

Store sauce in a covered container in refrigerator up to 3 days.

Chef's Tip: When reheating Rye Whiskey Sauce, use a moderate temperature so the egg in the sauce doesn't curdle.

Fig Pecan Pie

176

## FIG PECAN PIE

Yield: 6 to 8 servings

*Chef's Note: While at Commander's Palace, Creole Chef Floyd Bealer came to me with the idea of uniting two very Southern ingredients: figs and pecans. I turned his idea into a winning pie.*

3/4 cup sugar
1 tablespoon cornstarch
1 cup light corn syrup
1 1/2 teaspoons vanilla extract
3 eggs, slightly beaten
1 cup drained fig preserves
1/2 cup finely chopped dried figs
1 1/2 cups pecan pieces
1 (9-inch) unbaked pie shell
  (see recipe, page 177)

Preheat oven to 300 degrees.

Combine sugar and cornstarch in a medium bowl.

Add corn syrup and vanilla; mix well.

Stir in eggs, preserves, dried figs and pecans until thoroughly incorporated. Pour mixture into pie shell. Bake 1 hour, or until pie is set.

Chef's Tips: You're lucky if you have a neighbor with a fig tree. However, we're seeing fresh figs in local grocery stores. Home-made fig preserves are preferred. Check your grocery for a brand with some syrup. For the crowning glory, select either butter pecan ice cream or make your own fig ice cream with preserves swirled into vanilla bean ice cream. Some like to top the pie with Grand Marnier ice cream, or just chase the dessert with a shot of orange liqueur.

## PIE SHELL

Yield: 2 (9-inch) pie shells

*Chef's Note: My mother Gladys' pies were blue ribbon winners at the Howard County Fair in Missouri. Today friends beg to go home with me to eat one of her apple, cherry or gooseberry pies. We served the Brennan's of Houston interpretation of Mom's and Dad's mincemeat pie at the James Beard House in 1998. Naturally, the first step to a first rate pie is an impeccable crust.*

2½ cups all-purpose flour
¾ teaspoon salt
1 cup vegetable shortening
6 to 8 tablespoons ice cold water
2 (9-inch) pie pans

Place flour and salt in a large bowl; add shortening and work mixture with hands or pastry cutter just until shortening is incorporated and the size of dimes and nickels.

Add 6 tablespoons water and mix until dough just comes together. If needed, add additional water a teaspoon at a time.

Divide dough into 2 equal portions. Form into thick, round disc shapes. Wrap each in plastic wrap. Refrigerate until dough is firm.

On a clean surface, evenly roll out dough. Turn frequently so it does not stick to the counter. Roll from center out to the edges, until dough is an even 3/16-inch thickness and larger than the pie pan by 1 inch all around. Use flour to dust, as needed, under and on top of dough to keep it from sticking to surface or rolling pin.

Fold dough in half and carefully lay across half of pie pan, or roll dough onto the rolling pin. Gently unfold to cover and center in the pan with an edge overlap all the way around pan. Lightly pat dough down into pan. To form a fluted edge, double the overlapping edge up above the rim of the pan about 1 inch. With left index finger and thumb about an inch apart on the outside edge of shell, use right thumb or index finger and press the dough between the fingers on left hand, making connecting V or U shapes all the way around the pan.

May be frozen up to 1 month in a large zip-lock plastic bag.

Chef's Tips: When mixing flour and shortening, the less you mix, the flakier the crust will be. Flaky crusts are ideal for fruit pies. Mealy crusts are best for custard pies.

To repair an open crack or hole in a crust after it's in the pan, lightly moisten the area, patch it with another piece of dough and sprinkle flour on the area to dry up excess moisture.

Strawberry Shortcake

## STRAWBERRY SHORTCAKE

Yield: 6 servings

*Chef's Note: Shortcakes and strawberries double up in this most Southern of sweets. We like to think ours is what your mother would make with its layering of sugary shortcake, scarlet berries and voluptuous whipped cream.*

3 cups fresh strawberries, stems removed, divided
1 cup granulated sugar, divided
1/4 cup Grand Marnier (optional)

1 1/4 cups all-purpose flour
1 tablespoon baking powder
1/2 cup vegetable shortening
2 eggs
2 tablespoons milk
1 tablespoon almond extract
1 cup whipping cream
1 tablespoon sugar
1/4 teaspoon vanilla extract
1 tablespoon powdered sugar
6 fresh mint sprigs

In a blender or food processor, purée 1 cup strawberries, 1/2 cup sugar and Grand Marnier.

Depending on size, halve or quarter remaining 2 cups strawberries and add to puréed sauce; reserve chilled until ready to use.

Preheat oven to 375 degrees.

Combine flour, remaining 1/2 cup sugar and baking powder in a large bowl. Cut in shortening until mixture is crumbly.

Mix eggs, milk and almond extract in a small bowl. Add to crumbly mixture and stir with a wooden spoon until smooth.

Use a dessert spoon to spoon out 6 equal portions of dough onto an ungreased sheet pan.

Bake about 10 to 15 minutes, or until lightly browned and done; test with a toothpick. Reserve, keeping warm.

In a chilled bowl beat cream, 2 tablespoons sugar and vanilla extract until stiff peaks form; reserve in refrigerator until ready to use.

Slice shortcakes in half; place a bottom half on each plate and top with reserved strawberries and sauce. Garnish with a dollop of reserved whipped cream.

Place top half of shortcake over whipped cream; sift powdered sugar over top and garnish with a sprig of fresh mint.

Chef's Tips: Shortcake pairs with any fresh seasonal fruit like blackberries, blueberries, raspberries, mangoes, peaches, nectarines and more. Cook up a batch of Bananas Foster and serve it shortcake-style instead of with ice cream. Scoop a delectable ice cream flavor in place of the whipped cream.

## CHOCOLATE PRALINE CHEESECAKE

Yield: 1 (10-inch) cheesecake

*Chef's Note: Chocolate Praline Cheesecake is another example of the baking artistry of past Pastry Chef, Melissa Piper Reilly. Chocolate Praline Cheesecake is one dessert you'll never offer to share.*

Chocolate Crumb Crust
  (recipe follows)
40 individually wrapped caramels
1/4 cup evaporated milk
1 cup toasted pecan pieces

1 1/2 pounds cream cheese, softened
3/4 cup sugar
3 eggs
6 (1-ounce) squares semi-sweet chocolate, melted

Prepare Chocolate Crumb Crust; reserve.

Place unwrapped caramels and evaporated milk in a medium stainless steel bowl set over simmering water in a large sauce pan. Periodically stir until caramels melt and blend with the milk. When mixture begins to look like a thick caramel, remove from heat.

Pour caramel on top of reserved crust.

Immediately sprinkle pecans on top of caramel mixture.

Preheat oven to 325 degrees.

Using a hand mixer beat cream cheese in a large bowl until smooth.

Add sugar gradually and beat until fluffy, scraping down sides of bowl. Blend in eggs, one at a time, scraping down sides of bowl after each addition. Add chocolate to mixture; blend until incorporated.

Pour mixture on top of caramel-pecan filling.

Set springform pan on an 18-inch square of heavy-duty aluminum foil; crimp foil up sides of pan to prevent any moisture from seeping into crust.

Place pan in a water bath (see Chef's Tips below); bake 45 minutes, or until cheesecake is set in the center.

Cool cheesecake to room temperature, 1 to 2 hours before refrigerating.

Do not remove from springform pan until completely chilled, at least 4 hours or overnight.

Chef's Tips: Substitute this Chocolate Crumb Crust for a store-bought one in our Peanut Butter Fudge Pie (page 182).

To melt caramels and milk quickly, place them in a large glass bowl and microwave on 50-percent power.

A water bath (bain marie) is used to help control the heat and to ensure a smooth texture in delicate items like custards and cheesecakes. Set pan with food to be baked inside another larger pan; add hot water until it comes up to the level of the filling inside the baking pan. Be sure to check pan sizes before filling with food. A disposable aluminum baking pan set onto a sheet pan works well as the bain marie pan.

## CHOCOLATE CRUMB CRUST

1 cup graham cracker crumbs
2 tablespoons sugar
3 (1-ounce) squares semi-sweet chocolate, melted
3 tablespoons unsalted butter, melted

Mix graham cracker crumbs, sugar, chocolate and butter with a large spoon in a medium bowl until well combined.

Press mixture firmly into bottom of a 10-inch springform pan; set aside.

## KEY LIME TART

Yield: 1 (9-inch) Tart; 6 to 8 servings

*Chef's Note: End any meal in the tropics with this much-called-for finale, a legacy from our former Dessert Diva, Laura Crucet.*

1 recipe Coconut Sablèe Crust (recipe follows)
3 egg yolks
1 cup sweetened condensed milk
9 tablespoons freshly squeezed Key lime juice
2 egg whites
3 tablespoons sugar
Optional garnishes; sweetened whipped cream, lime slices, fresh raspberries and raspberry sauce

Prepare Coconut Sablè Crust; bake and reserve.

Preheat oven to 325 degrees. In a large bowl, whisk egg yolks, condensed milk and lime juice. Let stand; mixture will begin to thicken after a few minutes. Using a hand mixer, in another large bowl beat egg whites and sugar until peaks begin to appear around edge of bowl. Add egg white mixture to lime curd; gently fold together until thoroughly incorporated.

Pour mixture into baked tart shell; bake 15 minutes.

Remove from oven and cool to room temperature, about 30 minutes. Freeze at least 2 hours before cutting or serving.

Top each serving with a dollop of sweetened whipped cream crowned with a lime slice. Decorate the plate with fresh raspberries and a drizzle of raspberry sauce for color and flavor contrast.

Chef's Tips: Pasteurized egg whites can be substituted for the raw egg whites in this dessert. Fresh regular lime juice will work if you can't locate Key limes.

## COCONUT SABLÈ CRUST

Yield: 1 (9 x ¾-inch) tart shell

1 cup unsalted butter
½ cup powdered sugar
½ teaspoon vanilla extract
1½ cups unsifted all-purpose flour
½ cup shredded coconut

Using an electric mixer, cream butter, sugar and vanilla in a large bowl just until butter starts to soften.

Slowly add flour and mix until a soft dough forms. Blend in coconut.

Wrap dough in plastic wrap and chill in refrigerator until dough is firm, about 2 hours.

Roll out dough on a heavily floured surface to fit tart pan. Gently place dough in tart pan; trim top to fit.

Keep tart crust refrigerated until ready to bake.

Preheat oven to 325 degrees. Bake tart crust 10 minutes — do not let brown. Remove from oven and reserve until ready to fill.

Chef's Tip: When working with this dough, use plenty of flour so it doesn't stick to the surface. Handle dough sparingly to avoid melting the dough's butter. If you have trouble with the dough breaking apart as you place it in the tart pan, don't worry. A little cut, paste and press should fix the problem — just like the computer.

181

*"After a perfect meal, we are more susceptible to the ecstacy of love than any other time."*
*— Dr. Hans Bazli*

Key Lime Tart

## TRADITION IS BETTER

My dad is an old-fashioned cook. One day he brought me a splattered, piece of paper that was as fragile as the Dead Sea Scrolls. It was a tried-and-true Angel Food Cake recipe — there's no telling how long he's had it.

Not too long ago, he was searching for a cookbook that turned out to be an antique from the 1890s. I finally found the only one available on the Internet. A new cookbook just wouldn't do for him.

Peanut Butter Fudge Pie

## PEANUT BUTTER FUDGE PIE

Yield: 8 servings

*Chef's Note: To salute Houston's hosting of the 1992 Republican National Convention, I decided a Texas-themed pie was in order. Texas is the No. 2 peanut-producing state, so I teamed peanuts with elements of Commander's Palace Chocolate Sheba dessert. I nestled chocolate fudge on a layer of peanut butter in a cookie crust, mounded the result with whipped cream, showered it all with caramel and chocolate sauces — and the Mud Slinger Pie was born! Following the convention, we re-christened the Mud Slinger as Peanut Butter Fudge Pie for anyone with a "taste" for politics.*

3/4 cup smooth peanut butter, softened
1 (9-inch) prepared chocolate cookie crust
5 tablespoons unsalted butter, melted

3 tablespoons Kahlúa (optional)
8 ounces semi-sweet chocolate, melted
1/4 cup whipping cream
8 tablespoons sugar, divided
4 ounces pasteurized egg whites
Whipped cream, chocolate sauce, caramel sauce and chopped peanuts for garnish

Spread peanut butter over bottom of cookie crust, being careful not to crack the crust; set aside.

In a large bowl, fold butter and Kahlua into chocolate; set aside.

In another large bowl, whisk cream and 4 tablespoons sugar to soft peaks. Fold into chocolate.

In a medium bowl whip egg whites to soft peaks; add remaining 4 tablespoons sugar and whip to stiff peaks. Fold into chocolate mixture.

Spread mixture evenly over peanut butter in cookie crust. If you end up with extra filling, divide it into ramekins and top with whipped cream for a chef's treat.

Place pie in freezer 2 hours, or until pie is set. Prior to serving, transfer pie to refrigerator for thawing.

When ready to present to guests, decorate as desired with whipped cream, chocolate sauce, caramel sauce and chopped roasted peanuts.

**Chef's Tips:** Pasteurized eggs are usually found in the grocer's refrigerated section, close to the fresh eggs. Look for prepared cookie crusts on the baking aisle at the store.

Experiment with your choice of liqueur flavors for the pie filling.

With a large pastry bag and large star tip, pipe whipped cream in star shapes to cover top of the entire pie. A drizzling of chocolate and caramel sauces and topped with chopped, fresh-roasted peanuts complete the pie's sinful presentation. For easier cutting, run the knife under hot water between each cut.

## PRALINE PIE

Yield: 6 to 8 servings

*Chef's Note: We can never have enough pralines. Former Sous Chef Wylie Poundstone recommended a new baker who developed this Praline Pie with the same ingredients as our pralines, cooked down into a flaky pastry shell.*

1 cup whipping cream
1 cup sugar
2 cups finely chopped pecans
1 tablespoon praline liqueur
1 (9-inch) unbaked pie shell (page 177)
Butter pecan ice cream for garnish

Preheat oven to 325 degrees.

Heat cream and sugar in a heavy, medium saucepan over medium-high heat until mixture boils.

Remove pan from heat and cool 10 minutes. Stir in pecans and liqueur. Pour mixture into pie shell and bake 45 minutes, or until golden brown and pie is set.

Serve with a scoop of ice cream on the top or side.

**Chef's Tips:** When you read these ingredients and directions, you'll see it's as "easy as pie." I wish our regular pralines were this simple to make!

Think about choosing another favorite liqueur, such as Grand Marnier, in place of praline liqueur.

For buffets, picnics, holidays, hostess or other gifts, bake Praline Pie in a crust lined jellyroll pan, cut the finished product into diamond shapes, and you have Praline Pie Diamonds.

183

*"Food is to eat, not to hang on the wall."*
*— William Denton*

# OUR TEXAS CREOLE STORY

My family and our restaurants have always been New Orleanians. I know restaurants can't be New Orleanians, but I've always thought of them as citizens. New Orleanians are masters at having a grand time, extracting the most out of everyday life, as well as from celebrations. Although food plays a part of our normal routine, in my hometown it takes on a zest that is unrivaled. Our restaurants are that way as well. Some people see bread pudding. We see bread pudding souffle! It's all in the way you look at life and is a huge part of our cooking philosophy.

Our cuisine revolves around "terroir," a French term describing the blend of soul and climate that dictates what grows well in a given area. Creoles drew from the bounty of South Louisiana's bayous and rich alluvial soil. Thus, a refined, distinctive fare evolved, separate from the rural cooking of the Cajuns. Other people may not be able to differentiate between the two, but just say "New Orleans restaurant," and they'll know what you're talking about!

Brennan's of Houston began life as a New Orleans restaurant in Texas — a successful copy of the original. Great cooking and hospitality are very personal things though. Over time those who worked here contributed their own undeniable passion and influence. Since our cornerstone is to hire folks fanatical about the magic of food, the result means things weren't going to be static. Years back I realized we weren't just a New Orleans restaurant any more. What were we though?

The answer to that tough question is twofold. First, despite our Creole roots, salsas, chiles and other fresh ingredients crept onto our menu.

Second, regional cuisine came out of hiding. Instead of French and Italian, Southwestern and California cuisine became hot. Each area of the country rediscovered its own traditions and "terroir." Before you could say chervil, cilantro was in everything!

However, we weren't really Southwestern either. We were in Houston, located in Texas and dubbed the "Bayou City." Houston has a dual personality. We revel in being Texans, but are fiercely loyal to our local roots. Although Texans are a breed apart, Texans who live on the coast are different than those living in the Hill Country, the Valley, or the High Plains. The Gulf and all its bounty are as much a part of us as they are foreign to citizens elsewhere in our great state. Stephan Pyles' "New Texas Cuisine" states: "Texas, after all, is adjacent to Louisiana and shares the same seafood that helped make Cajun and Creole cooking famous." Stephan was talking about our "terroir."

You don't hear much about SouthEAST cuisine do you? Creole, Cajun, New Florida and Low Country may compose that region, but each has a unique "terroir." We have come to call ours Texas Creole. We think that sums up neatly the description of a New Orleans restaurant in Houston, Texas for almost 35 years.

— Alex Brennan-Martin

Airline Seafood
1841 Richmond Ave.
Houston, TX 77098
713-526-2351
www.airlineseafood.com
*Turtle meat, crabmeat, crawfish, fish
and other seafood products*

Anson Mills
2013 Greene St.
Columbia, SC 29205
or
3 Charlestown Rd.
Charleston, SC 29407
843-709-7399
www.ansonmills.com
*Fresh grits, antebellum grits,
coarse-style white and yellow grits,
Artisanal handmade polenta and
cornmeal*

186

Baumer Foods Inc.
4301 Tulane Ave.
New Orleans, LA 70119
504-482-5761 or 800-618-8667
*Crystal Hot Sauce, mustards, etc.*

Brennan's of Houston
3300 Smith St.
Houston, TX, 77006
713-522-9711
www.brennanshouston.com
*Source of Brennan's of Houston,
information, updates and other
products*

Broken Arrow Ranch
P.O. Box 530
Ingram, TX 78025
800-962-4263
www.brokenarrowranch.com
*Venison shanks and sausage,
wild boar and other game meats*

Chef Paul Prudhomme's
Magic Seasonings
P.O. Box 23342
New Orleans, LA 70183
800-457-2857 or 504-731-3590
www.chefpaul.com
*Creole seasonings, tasso ham,
andouille sausage*

Gourmet Ranch
4923 East Oak
Pasadena, TX 77503
281-998-4878 or 800-967-7514
www.helmutl@gourmetranch.com
*Demi-glacé, meats; beef, game, fowl
and many other great products*

www.LouisianaRadio.com, or
www.Louisianacajun.com
*Louisiana music to go with your
Creole cooking*

The Mozzarella Co.
2944 Elm St.
Dallas, TX 75226
800-798-2954 or 214-741-4072
www.mozzco.com
*Fresh mozzarella and other cheeses*

New Orleans Fish House
921 Dupre St.
New Orleans, LA 70125
800-839-3474
www.nofh.com
*Seafood*

New Orleans School of Cooking
and Louisiana General Store
524 St. Louis St.
New Orleans, LA 70130
800-237-4841
www.neworleanscooking.com
*Good source for many Louisiana
products: Zatarain's Creole mustard, crab and shrimp boils, Mardi
Gras decorations, coffee, rice, other
Creole and Cajun products*

Perrone's Progress Grocery
4512 Zenith St.
Metairie, LA 70001
866-455-3663 or 504-455-3663
www.progressgrocery.com
*Popcorn rice and Creole specialties*

The C.S. Steen Syrup Mill, Inc.
P.O. Box 339
Abbeyville, LA 70511
800-725-1654 or 337-893-1654
www.steensyrup.com
*Cane syrup and molasses*

Tabasco Country Store
Catalogue
McIlhenny Company
Avery Island, LA 70513
800-634-9599
www.tabasco.com
*Tabasco products*

source guide

# index

187

## D